EVATT FOUNDATION

Moving in the Open Daylight
Doc Evatt, an Australian at the United Nations

Ashley Hogan

SYDNEY UNIVERSITY PRESS

Published by SYDNEY UNIVERSITY PRESS

© Ashley Hogan and the Evatt Foundation 2008
© Sydney University Press 2008

Reproduction and Communication for other purposes
Except as permitted under the Act, no part of this edition may be
reproduced, stored in a retrieval system, or communicated in any form or
by any means without prior written permission. All requests for
reproduction or communication should be made to Sydney University
Press at the address below:

Sydney University Press
Fisher Library F03, University of Sydney, NSW 2006 AUSTRALIA
Email: info@sup.usyd.edu.au

National Library of Australia Cataloguing-in-Publication entry
Author: Hogan, Ashley.
Title: Moving in the Open Daylight: Doc Evatt, an Australian
at the United Nations / Ashley Hogan.
ISBN: 978-1-920899-28-8
Notes: Bibliography.
Subjects: Evatt, Herbert Vere, 1894–1965.
                 United Nations -- Officials and employees, Australian --
                 Biography.
                 Australia -- Foreign relations -- 20th century.
                 Australia -- History -- 20th century.
Other Authors/Contributors: Herbert Vere Evatt Memorial Foundation.
Dewey Number: 994.04

Front cover photograph courtesy of the State Library of New South Wales

"As I see it, there are only three languages in which a nation can speak internationally – the language of force; the language of deception, hidden purpose, and secret agreement; and the language of the common man moving in the open daylight. Some nations have preferred and still prefer the first two ... The third has not yet been tried fully and universally, and some nations still do not seem to believe in it. But so long as there is a Labor Government in Australia that is the language in which our viewpoint will be stated."

> – *Dr H. V. Evatt, Evatt Collection: UN Miscellaneous, Flinders University, Adelaide.*

Contents

Foreword
The Honourable Justice Michael Kirby AC CMG

Dr Herbert Vere Evatt was an outstanding Australian. He was also a highly influential internationalist. As we celebrate the sixtieth anniversary of the Universal Declaration of Human Rights (UDHR), adopted by the General Assembly of the United Nations on 10 December 1948 when Evatt was President, it is fitting that Australians, and all people, should reflect on his contributions to humanity both at home and abroad.

In his lifetime, Evatt was a highly controversial figure in Australia. The greatest prize to which he aspired, to be elected Prime Minister of Australia, eluded him. Yet in truth, there were few Australians of the 20th century who stacked up more achievements of lasting benefit to the nation and the world.

A product of the public education system at Fort Street High School in Sydney, Evatt won bursaries to Sydney University and graduated with one of the most brilliant academic records ever attained. He became a brave and imaginative advocate. He was a scholar and writer of lasting importance. He then became the youngest person ever appointed a Justice of the High Court. In the dark days of war, he resigned as a judge and sought election to the Federal Parliament in a marginal seat. His election led to his serving as Federal Attorney-General and Minister for External Affairs at a critical time for the survival of the Commonwealth. It was in that period that he took a leading part in the creation of the United Nations Organisation, the adoption of its Charter, the establishment of the agencies and the initiation of the UDHR which later became the foundation for the International Bill of Rights.

After he lost governmental office in Australia in December 1949, Evatt's contributions to liberty were not concluded. Against party opposition and all odds, he fought the *Communist Party Dissolution Act* 1950 in the High Court of Australia. He convinced the High Court to declare the Act unconstitutional. He then contested the referendum that sought to overcome that court decision by amendment of the Constitution. He saved Australia from a serious blot on its liberal democracy. Political passions frustrated, he resigned as Leader of the Opposition and was appointed Chief Justice of New South Wales. From that office he soon resigned, broken and ill and died not long after.

By the time this last appointment came to him, Evatt was already demonstrating mental failure. It was all too evident to the lawyers, including myself, who observed this intellectual giant in the Banco Court in Sydney, deteriorating before their eyes. It was this deterioration that left a painful memory, as enemies and critics circled to assail his reputation. Some of their criticisms were doubtless valid. Especially by the end, Evatt was like *Lear*: unpredictable, enigmatic, suspicious, disordered. Even at the peak of his powers, his brilliance caused him to work in ways that seemed chaotic to more orderly and pedestrian minds.

Yet as this work on Evatt's contributions to the post-World War II legal order clearly demonstrates, his heroic work schedule and engagement with so many others won him deep admiration. More importantly, they contributed greatly to three vital elements of the United Nations system. These were the role within the United Nations of the smaller states, particularly in the General Assembly; the functions within the United Nations of the agencies where most of the good work of the Organisation is done; and the provision to the United Nations of a distinctive moral foundation, in the form of the International Bill of Rights and the Trusteeship Council based upon the fiduciary obligations of equity law that he had learned as a young lawyer. That idea was to bring all the trusteeships of the United Nations to independence, which was achieved by 1994.

What other Australian of the 20th century can boast of equivalent contributions to the entire world? In the big picture of humanity's survival and the protection of our species from destruction through conflict, genocide, nuclear proliferation, prejudice and inequality, Evatt's activities on the world stage transcended purely national achievements. The flaws of personality and the chaos of his work methods, the rumpled suits, the vanity, the press clippings and the gravelly voice, fade in memory with the years. It is the institutions that people leave, and that sometimes survive, that become their most lasting human legacies. This monograph shows the importance of Evatt's institutional contributions to the United Nations. Of course, the Organisation is imperfect and it needs ongoing reform. But we have to ask what would have happened if the United Nations had not existed as the forum for the voice of humanity.

When the people of Australia voted down the attempt of Prime Minister R. G. Menzies to amend the Constitution to afford powers to the Federal Parliament to dissolve the Australian Communist Party and place civil burdens on communists, Evatt told his parliamentary party colleagues that it had been more important to defeat that referendum than to win government in a series of federal elections. History suggests that this was a correct assessment. So, equally, it can be said that it was more important in the big picture that Evatt contributed, as he did, to shaping the new world legal order at a critical and vulnerable moment in the history of humanity than that he should have achieved his goal of election as Australia's Prime Minister.

So here is a tale of epic proportions of a man, flawed as we all are, who was an internationalist, a libertarian, a fine lawyer and judge, and a most energetic public officer when these qualities were specially needed. With the passage of time his flaws and mortal weaknesses recede in memory and significance. His perception of global institutions and of the idea that an

Australian could, and should, play a part in shaping them leaves to us, who are left, a legacy that is inspiring and encouraging for later generations. The global mission that he accepted is by no means complete. But Herbert Vere Evatt left a big mark. Overwhelmingly this was for the benefit of humanity. This account reminds us of his achievements. They are very great indeed.

High Court of Australia
Canberra
1 October 2008

1. Introduction

Herbert Vere Evatt, 'Bert' to his family and 'Doc' to everyone else, is one of Australia's best-known political figures. He held seats in parliament at both the state and federal levels and sat on both the High Court and the Supreme Court of New South Wales (NSW). He was the Minister for External Affairs during World War II and post-war reconstruction. After Ben Chifley's death in 1951, he became Federal Parliamentary Leader of the Australian Labor Party (ALP) during some of the most trying and dramatic days in its history.

As leader, Evatt presided over a party trapped in opposition by internal divisions. Some historians argue that Evatt's own decisions and behaviour cost Labor dearly, from giving Robert Menzies a 'wedge' by opposing the referendum to ban the Communist Party in 1951, to his personal appearance at the Petrov Royal Commission and his confrontational attitude during the Split of 1954.[1] Others hold that Labor's position in the 1950s could not have been repaired by any leader and characterise Evatt's fight against anti-communism in Australia's political culture as a courageous defence of civil liberties.[2]

Evatt's position on the Australian political stage often obscures his international achievements. Before he became Labor leader, he was John Curtin's and then Ben Chifley's Minister for External Affairs. He held that position from 1941 to Labor's defeat at the 1949 election. Under his guidance, Australia developed an independent foreign policy based on Labor's priorities of national security through international justice. Although foreign minister of a small and not particularly powerful country, he played a significant, even crucial, role in the formation of the United Nations and the foundation of the post-World War II international order. His contribution and leadership were recognised with his election to the position of President of the General Assembly of the United Nations on 21 September 1948. On 10 December 1948, while Evatt held that post, the General Assembly adopted and proclaimed the Universal Declaration of Human Rights.

Doc Evatt is often regarded as one of the great eccentrics on the Australian and international political scene. He could be abrasive, neurotic, petulant and egocentric.[3] Yet, as Ross McMullin writes, 'he could be exhilarating, unpredictably endearing, and admirably courageous and tenacious on matters of principle'.[4] He was indubitably able, with a tremendous capacity for work. Whether despite or because of his abrasiveness and lack of polish, Evatt successfully forced his way into the inner circles of the world's post-war negotiations and left an imprint that endured for decades.

Evatt and his time

Herbert Vere Evatt was born on 30 April 1894 in East Maitland, NSW, the fifth of eight sons (two of whom died before his birth). Evatt's father, John Evatt, a publican, died in 1901, when Evatt was only seven years old. His mother Jeanie tried for a few years to keep the hotel going, but eventually moved from Maitland to Milsons Point in Sydney, closer to family support. Evatt did well in school, winning a bursary and a scholarship. He went to Sydney University, first to study Arts and then Law. He was active in university politics and very successful academically, winning the University Medal (twice). These years were shadowed by the death of two of his brothers in World War I.[5]

In 1918 Evatt was admitted to the bar and in 1920 he married Mary Alice Sheffer, a marriage that would be life-long and one of strong mutual support. In 1920, Evatt also acted as counsel for the government in the Edmonds Royal Commission into the victimisation of railroad workers who had taken part in the 1917 General Strike in NSW. Evatt distinguished himself by his passionate concern for the denial of natural justice by the internal investigative processes of the railways. The report of the Commission was not acted upon, showing Evatt that change was not necessarily the province of the courts. He represented more and more union and labour cases in the following years and joined the ALP. He worked to secure preselection for the state seat of Balmain, becoming secretary and then president of his local branch. In 1924 he was awarded a doctorate of laws for a thesis on 'The Royal Prerogative'. In the same year he became the chairman of the ALP's Fighting Platform Committee, which was responsible for drafting the policy statement the party would take to the election. In 1925, after a vigorous campaign, he won the seat. In subsequent years he successfully combined parliamentary work with his labour law practice.[6]

Disillusionment with NSW Premier Jack Lang and increasing policy and personality conflicts with senior party figures led Evatt to leave parliament in 1930. Later that year he became the youngest judge ever appointed to the High Court. His judgements from this time are marked by his concern for liberal and humane principles. In August 1940 the Federal Executive of the ALP unanimously agreed to invite Evatt to be the endorsed Labor candidate in the seat of Barton. Held by the United Australia Party (UAP) for the previous nine years, it was a winnable but not a safe seat. Evatt won. Labor did not.[7]

At the beginning of World War II the Australian Labor Party was coming out of a period of opposition exacerbated by a debilitating split. John Curtin's job in uniting the party was far from easy.[8] When war broke out, the leader of the UAP and prime minister was Robert Menzies. At the 1940 election, the UAP government survived only with the support of two independent members of parliament and Menzies sought a coalition wartime government with Labor's John Curtin.[9] Eager for a ministry, Evatt supported the idea of an all-party national government. Curtin opposed the proposal and Evatt accused him of timidity. It might be more accurate to say that Curtin wished Labor to govern in its own right. After Menzies' own party turned on him and the independent MPs turned on the UAP government, John Curtin's Labor government took power in October 1941. Evatt became Attorney-General and Minister for External Affairs and Australia was plunged into a struggle for national survival.[10]

For Curtin's cabinet, bearing memories of the horrors of World War I and the Great Depression, the need for not only victory but also long-term change was clear. The three great crises of Australia's first half-century can be seen in every preoccupation of the party at this time and in Evatt himself: abhorrence of war and a determination that it be avoided wherever possible; a determination to provide security for the nation; and an abiding desire to turn aside the ravages of poverty and unemployment.[11] For Australian Labor Party politicians in the 1940s, the search for solutions was not an abstract exercise. In their own electorates, in their own families, in their own lives, they had seen the devastation of war and of economic disaster.

The Curtin government was immediately tested with the fall of Singapore in February 1942. Many Australian troops were taken prisoner and the nation's territorial security seemed to be under immediate threat. Curtin insisted that Australian forces on their way to the Netherlands East Indies be diverted to defend the homeland, not sent to Burma as British Prime Minister Winston Churchill wanted.[12] These episodes stretched the relationship between Britain and Australia.[13] Nonetheless, even as Curtin was telling citizens that 'Australia looks to America' in 1941, the government still saw the nation as part of the Commonwealth.[14]

This was a defining time for Australian foreign policy. Christopher Waters argues that it was the first development of a distinctive sovereign foreign policy 'in both substance and style', a policy that emphasised 'the importance of the effective participation of smaller nations, of regional defence in the

Pacific, and of the improvement of the welfare of the native peoples of the Pacific and South East Asia'.[15] In January 1944, Australia and New Zealand formalised their agreement on these priorities with the ANZAC Pact — a co-operation which would become the basis for many policy positions at the United Nations Conference on International Organisation (UNCIO) at San Francisco in 1945, the conference which created the United Nations.[16]

Labor's position in government was secured with a conclusive election victory in 1943. Although there was general consistency in Labor's approach to the problems of post-war organisation, there were still differences in opinion within the government, including between Evatt and Curtin. In May 1944 Curtin travelled to London for the Commonwealth Prime Ministers' Conference without Evatt. Curtin 'displayed a much more moderate enthusiasm for the proposed International Organisation' and placed much more emphasis on the British Commonwealth.[17] Evatt reminded him in cables from Canberra that it was Australia's position, contrary to the United Kingdom's position, that the International Organisation should *not* be run on a three or four power basis and there should be a 'proper place for the voice and interest of the smaller powers'.[18]

Nicolas Greet suggests that Curtin might have decided to exclude Evatt from the Conference because of the incompatibility of their views and the perception that the Doc's manner and manners had a negative effect on Australia's international standing.[19] This was a difference in emphasis that did not signify a substantial difference in policy. In October 1944 Evatt told the House of Representatives that *both* consultation and joint action within the British Commonwealth *and* the exercise of 'Australia's distinct international status' would have to be used to achieve the country's foreign policy goals.[20] Waters describes this developing policy stance, which came to fruition during the post-war Chifley government, as being 'moulded by liberal internationalist principles, while British policy remained wedded to realist traditions'.[21]

At the same time as the Curtin government was developing foreign policy priorities, plans for post-war organisation — both domestic and international — were emerging. Labor Party priorities such as a commitment to full employment shaped these plans. As Ken Buckley, Barbara Dale and Wayne Reynolds have written,

> members of the Curtin Government were much concerned about post-war prospects. As part of the labour movement, they entertained a vision of creating in Australia a society affording a better life for the people. In particular, they were determined to prevent reversion to the circumstances of the depression of the 1930s. These Labor views provided a broad framework for articulation of reconstruction plans.[22]

In Curtin's own words, in his July 1943 policy speech:

> This government's policy of full development of resources, full employment of man-power and full provision for social security is a basis not only for Australian reconstruction, but for a stable and peaceful commonwealth of all nations ... In banishing want, we shall have gone far to free the world from fear ... I give you the Labor Government's policy in a phrase — victory in war, victory in peace. On that we stand inflexible, for a lost peace would be marked by horrors of starvation, unemployment, misery and hardship no less grievous than the devastation of war.[23]

Evatt echoed these sentiments in an article published in the Sydney *Daily Telegraph* a month later: 'we also have a duty to assist in making practical the United Nations' objective of "freedom from want"'.[24]

Years later, in 1949, Chifley would say in his famous 'Light on the Hill' speech that the 'great objective' of the Labor Party was 'the betterment of mankind — not only here but anywhere we may give a helping hand'. Both the prime ministers in whose cabinets Evatt served expressed, in their different ways, the same policy principles — those Evatt would take to the United Nations Conference in San Francisco in 1945.

The international background

What we know as the *First* World War was, to those who lived through it, the *Great* War, the war to end all wars. In its immediate aftermath, the victors formed the League of Nations, intended to prevent such a cataclysm happening again.

There were flaws inherent in the League's structure: it worked by unanimity on all but procedural issues, there were few options for resolving disputes under the League Covenant, and disregard of League reports or recommendations produced a range of automatic consequences, up to military action.[25] The outbreak of World War II demonstrated the League's inability to secure international peace. The response by a great many politicians around the world was not to abandon the concept but to immediately start considering what might replace it.

The replacement body would have to resolve both the structural issues and the issues of *scope* that had lead to the League's failure. Franklin Roosevelt's ringing phrases from his 'Four Freedoms' State of the Union address in 1941 — freedom of speech, freedom of religion, freedom from want, freedom from fear — encapsulated this broader agenda. Roosevelt was no lonely visionary. His words were adopted with enthusiasm by Evatt in his first parliamentary speech as Minister for External Affairs:

international peace can be maintained only through international justice, and the four great freedoms, freedom of speech, freedom of religion, freedom from fear, freedom from want, are meaningless unless they are enjoyed not in one or two countries but, as President Roosevelt insists, everywhere in the World.[26]

In Australia, the Curtin government, gaining office in the teeth of a desperate national struggle for survival and in the aftermath of a crushing Depression, was constructing a new nation in the depth of the war.

Addressing the listeners of the Sydney radio station 2UE as Attorney-General and Minister for External Affairs in January 1943, Evatt summarised the tension between the joint aims:

We fully recognise the need to plan and prepare for the post-war period so that the objectives of economic security and security of employment may be attained. These preparations are being made, and Mr Chifley has recently been appointed Minister for Post War Reconstruction. Yet all our plans, yes all our hopes too, will vanish if the Japanese are able to launch heavy attacks upon our beloved homeland.[27]

In 1942, Evatt had expressed similar sentiments to the British Labour Party Conference, saying: 'As the Labour Movement is clearly right in its intense concentration on the war, it is equally right in its desire to guard us all against disasters similar to those which followed victory in the last war'.[28]

The perception that the failure of the League to secure economic security contributed to the suffering of the Great Depression and to World War II contributed in turn to the determination of Evatt and his colleagues to ensure any post-war organisation would address a broad conception of security. A generation of politicians and leaders had survived World War I when they were young, losing friends and, in Evatt's case, family. Faced with another vast and catastrophic conflict, their reaction was not resignation but determination. The United Nations was born of equal parts hope and desperation. It was created by men and women determined to 'save the world from the scourge of war'.[29]

2. The birth of the UN

The failure of the League of Nations in 1939 did not mean that politicians and officials around the world turned their back on the idea of a body to facilitate peaceful solutions to conflict. Quite the reverse.[1] As politicians and statesmen considered what might replace the League, lessons learned from its failure were incorporated into their thinking.[2] The need for the 'great powers' of the world to be active participants was evident. For the smaller powers, the questions of avoiding domination and balancing sovereignty with enforcement remained crucial.[3]

Early indications of the issues that any world organisation would have to face became clearer with events such as the Cairo Conference in 1943, where Churchill, Roosevelt and Chiang-Kai-Shek decided on the post-war disposition of Japanese-occupied islands in the Pacific without consultation. Evatt responded with the rapid negotiation and conclusion of the Australia-New Zealand Agreement, declaring the right of both countries to be involved in post-war decision making and armistices.[4] The Australasian nations would also consult and reach agreement on principles prior to the British Commonwealth discussions of the proposals for the United Nations.[5]

Between August and October 1944, at Dumbarton Oaks in Washington, representatives of the United States, the Soviet Union, the United Kingdom and China began to plan out the proposed international organisation.[6] This was followed in February 1945 by the Yalta Conference, where Roosevelt, Stalin and Churchill agreed on a joint position on many of the vexed issues of the new international organisation. The most crucial would be the right of the great powers to veto action by the new organisation. Ultimately this would take the form of the representation by the five most powerful victors in World War II (the United States, the United Kingdom, the USSR, China and France) as permanent members of the United Nations Security Council, with the right to individually and unilaterally veto any Council action.

Despite both Curtin and Evatt expressing the opinion that Australia should be involved in the planning of the new organisation from its inception, the country had hardly any involvement in these early stages. This raised the stakes for Australia at the San Francisco Conference. As Bill Hudson has written:

> If Australia wanted to make a mark, it would have to be at the San Francisco Conference and this meant, in turn, that Australia and other like-minded small powers would go to San Francisco with expectations very different from those of the great powers. For Australia, the Dumbarton Oaks and Yalta texts would comprise only 'a basis for discussion' and the conference would be seen as a constitutional convention; for the great powers, the texts were to be discussed and explained but not lightly amended, and for them the conference would be an exercise in consultation.[7]

This was not the only likely conflict. There was a range of opinions concerning the potential usefulness, the structure and the scope of the proposed international organisation.

Early in the war, in June 1941, a number of the Allied nations met in London and signed the St James Palace Declaration, which mentioned economic and social security only as the consequence of being relieved of the menace of aggression.[8] Evatt saw economic and social security as the precondition for peace, arguing in 1943 that no system of security 'can be permanent unless it has an adequate basis in economic justice'.[9] In 1945 he told an audience at the University of California:

> Lasting world peace is not a negative but a positive concept, for peace is not merely the absence of war ... The truth is that real stability in the post-war world can be achieved only by carefully building an organisation

that will do its utmost to assure to the peoples of the world a full opportunity of living in freedom from want as well as in freedom from external aggression.[10]

To some degree, these different opinions were represented within the Australian government. Hudson argues that while Evatt perceived the United Nations as an opportunity to shape and improve the post-war world, John Curtin viewed the body more narrowly, concerned mostly with collective security in a more traditional sense.[11]

Curtin decided to send both Doc Evatt and Frank Forde — Deputy Prime Minister and Minister for the Army — to the San Francisco Conference, and the 'assistants and consultants' appointed to accompany them were weighted towards the army, along with representatives of interest groups and social movements (including the only woman on the Australian delegation, Jessie Street).[12] Evatt, however, was able to pick his own 'advisers' and he chose experts close to him: Paul Hasluck, John Burton, Keith Waller and William Forsyth from the Department of External Affairs in Canberra, Alan Watt and J. B. Brigden from the Australian legation in Washington, and Kenneth Bailey and L. F. Crisp. According to Hudson, '[i]t was these advisers' presence and quality which were to allow Evatt first to dominate the Australian delegation and then to emerge as one of the luminaries of the conference'.[13] Both Evatt and Forde later claimed they had been told by Curtin that they would lead the Australian delegation. Hudson concludes that Curtin told them both at different times they would lead, while John Plant suggests that Curtin assumed Forde, as Deputy Prime Minister, would be understood to be the leader.[14] Whatever the cause of the disagreement, it would lead to conflict within the delegation, bitterly expressed by Evatt in cablegrams home, although this did not impinge on the Australian performance.[15]

The British Commonwealth meeting in April 1945 was supposed to resolve issues so the countries could present a united front. But 'the exchange of views became an argument, and that argument revealed much about Evatt's belief and policies and strengthened his determination to present independent views at San Francisco'.[16] Most significantly, the right of the five great powers to veto action or decisions by the Security Council emerged as a point of contention at this meeting. Greet suggests that earlier correspondence with former prime minister and now Australian High Commissioner in London, Stanley Bruce, demonstrates both that Evatt was already aware of the problems such a veto would cause the new international organisation, and that he already accepted that the proposed United Nations would founder before it could be launched if the major international powers refused to participate.

With this issue unresolved, the San Francisco Conference began on 25 April 1945. There were 282 delegates from 50 countries, with 1500 staff and a secretariat of 1000 to translate the documents. Delegations ranged in size from three in the case of some small states to 175 from the United States, with the Australian group of 25 comparable in size to the delegations of other nations of similar size and status.[17] More than 2500 reporters attended. The principal committees on the General Assembly, the Security Council and the World Court were open to the public. Twelve other committees finalising the draft charter and resolving disagreements did their work without an audience.[18] By the end of the conference many of these committees were meeting twice a day, meaning that there were nine or ten meetings each day.[19] Each member of the Australian delegation, Evatt later wrote, attended 'as many committees as physically possible' so that everyone was familiar with the workings of the conference as a whole.[20] The Australians evolved a system of 'continuous reporting' which enabled Evatt to be on the spot when most required, fully informed of the issues at hand – leading to the joke that there were in fact 'ten Evatts' at the conference.[21]

Evatt arrived in San Francisco with a distinct agenda – an agenda with different but complementary items. This agenda was the result of a 'consistent evolution even if the process was somewhat hurried in its final stages'.[22] He was determined to make changes to the Charter that would improve the procedures and democratise the structures of the proposed United Nations Organisation; he was determined to expand its scope beyond the simple military security covered by the League, to a more expansive view of international security that included addressing the social and economic causes of conflict; he was determined that the rule of law should replace the brute force of power in international relations; he was committed to multilateralism and diplomacy in conflict resolution; and he was determined to establish Australia's independent stance in the world of international diplomacy.[23] Without success in the first of these aims, the others would have been impossible — while his final goal, Australia's independent position in world affairs, was cemented by his persistence in pursuit of the other goals.

The Australian proposals at San Francisco can be summarised thus:

1. To include the rule of law and the promotion of justice in the purposes of the United Nations and the principles guiding the Security Council and require the maximum employment of the Permanent Court in determining the legal aspects of international disputes.
2. To require members to recognise the jurisdiction of the International Court of Justice.
3. To require a pledge from all members to respect the territorial integrity and political independence of other members.
4. To strengthen the Security Council by giving it initiative and responsibility in securing agreements with members on military contributions, and by requiring that its membership be limited to those powers who have proved themselves able and willing to carry out substantial security responsibilities.

5. To exclude the 'veto' of the permanent members from all arrangements relating to the peaceful settlement of disputes and to confine such a veto to decisions involving the application of economic and military sanctions.
6. To require members to pledge themselves to take action both national and international for the purpose of securing for all peoples, including their own, improved labour standards, economic advancement, employment for all, and social security.
7. To elevate the Economic Council into a principal organ of the world organisation.
8. To give the General Assembly a wider jurisdiction over and a full share in the general work of the organisation, and in particular to vest the Assembly with power to prevent situations from becoming 'frozen' in the Security Council as had occurred in the League.
9. To lay down the principle that the purpose of administration of all dependent territories is the welfare and development of the native peoples of all such territories, and to place an obligation on nations controlling particular dependent territories.
10. To prevent the possibility of a single great power vetoing amendments to the constitution.
11. To ensure that the wide powers of the organisation could not be used to interfere with matters of domestic jurisdiction.
12. To ensure that inactivity on the part of the Security Council could not prevent the implementation of regional defence measures.[24]

The 'content' aspect of Australia's agenda — extending the United Nations to address the broadest range of social, economic, and rights issues — will be the subject of later chapters. But to address those issues, Evatt first had to make sure the United Nations was the right *kind* of organisation. His efforts to do so would secure him a prominent place in the ranks of world statesmen and change the shape and course of the United Nations.

Greet reports Paul Hasluck as giving Evatt credit for nearly the whole of Australia's achievements at the UNCIO and cites the assessment by P. G. Edwards that there is 'no doubt that from April to June 1945 Australian foreign policy was what Evatt said it was', adding that '[n]o other man has dominated the making of Australian foreign policy for a substantial period quite so single-handedly, except perhaps Hughes at Versailles'.[25] Norman Harper and David Sissons describe Evatt as:

a man of great intellect and dominant personality, [who] subsequently emerged as one of the outstanding figures of the Conference, the champion of the smaller powers. A liberal socialist and a former member of the Australian High Court, he brought to the Conference a passionate conviction of the need for morality in international affairs, a sense of mission, and a belief in the need for world government by gradual stages. These were combined with a devotion to legal processes and a humourless determination to establish democratic principles as the basis for the conduct of international relations.[26]

Plant remarks on the 'aggressiveness and force' of Australia's posture at San Francisco, an aggressiveness and force that other delegates might have been forgiven for confusing with Evatt's own posture.[27]

Evatt and his advisers thrived on the committee system at San Francisco. Well prepared and with a consistent and comprehensive agenda, 'Evatt was the most formidable and successful representative of the small and middle powers at San Francisco'.[28] By the end of the conference, the pace of work was crushing — an average of ten meetings a day, in morning, afternoon and evening sessions, with about 350 working meetings of commissions, committees and subcommittees held during the course of the Conference.[29] Evatt's stamina under such a workload was one factor in the Australian delegation's success.

Also critical was the election of Australia to the Executive Committee. This also meant membership of the Co-ordination Committee 'which prepared the final draft of the Charter. As a result of this election, Australia was closely associated with the great powers in the managing of the business of the conference and overcoming the difficulties that arose'.[30] Membership of the executive and agenda committees of any conference, often overlooked, gives control over the subject and direction of discussions. Evatt and Forde's report on the San Francisco Conference noted:

> One of the most notable successes of Australia at the Conference was to obtain appointment to the Executive Committee and hence to the Co-ordination Committee as well. These appointments helped considerably to establish our status at the Conference and afforded an exceptional opportunity to make a major contribution to the work of the Conference. The position which the Australian delegation established for itself was in a large measure due to the manner in which we discharged our duties as a member of the Executive Committee.[31]

According to Plant, after Evatt began to attend meetings of the Executive Committee as Australia's representative, he dominated the proceedings through personality and legal ability, and made himself the man who had to be pleased to get agreement from the small and medium powers at the Conference.[32]

The small and medium nations became Australia's allies — and Evatt's voting bloc — as the Conference progressed. Alan Renouf attributes Evatt's success at San Francisco to both 'his remarkable personal qualities' and 'his mobilization and leadership of the smaller powers. [Evatt] convinced them that they had diplomatic muscle, especially if they acted in unison'.[33] Evatt's championing of the interests of the smaller powers may have been partly opportunistic. But as Kenneth Bailey, who became Commonwealth Solicitor-General in 1946, said of Evatt: 'His instinct was always to support the underdog'.[34] Thomas Smith draws parallels between Evatt's *international* position and his actions in the domestic arena: '[i]n national politics and in world councils he fought aggressively for the little man and for the small country'.[35]

Evatt's dislike of power politics can be seen as part of this aspect of his character, his emphasis on democracy and rules stemming from the belief that these are the things which protect the rights of the weak from the depredations of the strong. To quote Renouf, he 'could not abide power politics. It was a form of diplomacy that grated on his liberalism, that was undemocratic (it would not give Australia a fair go) and that had been discredited by history'.[36] Power politics would always exclude small and medium countries like Australia from influence and effective participation in international affairs. The liberal internationalist principles which informed the foreign policy of the Curtin and Chifley Labor governments enabled Australia to play a larger role.[37]

Evatt staked a clear claim to this ground when Australia opposed the incorporation of the amendments by the great powers into the Dumbarton Oaks document before amendments from other countries were considered. 'Evatt immediately said it would be "a very wrong procedure" to treat the amendments of any power or group of powers as the basic document'.[38] He fought a long battle in the committees to have the amendments all considered equally, and if possible at the same time. This opposition to preferential treatment had several implications: the assertion that the conference might have begun with the Dumbarton Oaks document but that the United Nations now belonged to all nations; the constant emphasis that good outcomes could only follow good procedure that was a hallmark of Evatt's approach; and the political strategy of early demonstration to smaller and middling nations that Australia would defend their interests to the great powers.

Australia continued to assert a distinctly independent status and posture in the procedural debates, going against both America and Britain. Evatt's tough fight over procedural outcomes may indeed, as Plant suggests, have been motivated by a desire to demonstrate independence and stake a claim.[39] Yet Evatt's emphasis on procedural rather than power politics and his use of judicial ideas remained consistent throughout his involvement in the United Nations – a part of his defence of small and medium powers against the brute force of the great powers. The importance Evatt placed on procedural issues was not a distraction from policy or ideology. Evatt came from a political party structure where procedure and rules, where membership of the agenda committee and the exact procedures for voting and vetos, were the air breathed for those active in the party — and the way in which policy aims were achieved. However much we may wish to see Evatt as above such squalid party politics, he was a politician who had won preselection — twice — in the toughest school of Australian politics, the NSW ALP. He survived the enmity of Jack Lang and saw the NSW branch of the ALP tear itself apart throughout the 1930s, until finally the anti-Lang forces were able to bring both superior numbers and the party rules to bear in 1939.[40] These experiences would teach anyone the importance of well-written rules and dependable votes. In San Francisco, Evatt fought two major procedural fights — *against* the Security Council veto, and *in favour of* broadening the ambit of the General Assembly. The former he lost. The second he won.

The great powers had agreed before the Conference that their blueprint for the new world organisation would be dominated by a Security Council in which they had a comprehensive veto power.[41] 'Australia led the charge to modify the Yalta formula and prevent the veto from being exercised against attempts at peaceful settlement'.[42] While Evatt was not the only representative of small and middle powers to fight the veto, he was the 'most effective critic of the veto at San Francisco'.[43] Evatt's position was that the great powers should only be able to veto economic or military sanctions against themselves.[44] This was, as David Lee and Edward Luck both argue, a concession that Evatt realised he had to make to keep the great powers involved in the United Nations.[45]

Evatt and the New Zealand representative led the last-ditch effort to exclude the veto from discussions related to peaceful settlement by defining them as procedural matters over three days of vigorous debate. They lost that vote 10 to 20 with 15 abstentions. It is generally agreed by historians that the abstainers supported the amendment in principle — but the threat by the great powers that there would be no United Nations without the veto carried the day.[46] John Burton recalled that Evatt himself realised that the veto was the price of keeping the great powers involved in the United Nations and that he was relieved to have lost that crucial vote.[47] The ultimate outcome was that 'a party to a dispute could not block discussion and proposals by the Security Council for peaceful settlement, but beyond that one of the permanent members could veto proposals for action'.[48] This compromise may have been necessary but Evatt's position would be vindicated by experience, as Roberts and Kingsbury note: 'After 1945, the ambitious scheme for collective security in Chapter VII of the UN Charter was not implemented. The most obvious reason was the inability of the Permanent Members of the Security Council to reach agreement across the Cold War Divide.'[49] By 1948, Evatt was telling the Australian Institute of Political Science Winter Forum that, '[d]aily, it becomes increasingly clear that differences between the United States on the one hand and the Soviet Union on the other hand are affecting all aspects of international affairs' and 'there is now almost a complete lack of co-operation amongst the Big Powers'.[50]

Evatt then carried his fight against the veto to the question of amendments to the United Nations Charter. He argued against the right of the great powers to veto any such amendments. Evatt argued that amendments should be carried

when successive General Assemblies carried them by two-thirds majorities and when at least three of the five permanent members concurred on each occasion. Evatt reasoned that, if the great powers were unable to block reform of the Charter, the way would be left open for the creation of a world organisation in which all the great powers, the strongest members of international society, would be subject, like the small and middle powers, to effective international pressure.[51]

He may have been influenced by his own experience as Attorney-General, finding the Australian Constitution difficult to change with the failure of Labor's *Post-war Reconstruction and Democratic Rights* referendum in 1944.[52] He and other delegates concerned about the veto did manage 'to insert a provision for a General Conference, to be held no later than the tenth annual session of the General Assembly, to review the provisions of the Charter'.[53] By then, however, the Cold War had hardened positions and there was no possibility of real change or reform.

Evatt's next battleground was the General Assembly. The great powers, while designing a Security Council that would control action and which they could control, deliberately designed a weak Assembly that would be no challenge to the Council's authority. A key limitation on the General Assembly as conceived in the Dumbarton Oaks proposals was that, while it could discuss principles and questions, it could not make recommendations on specific cases or matters before the Security Council.[54] Evatt's counter-argument was that the Dumbarton Oaks proposals did not recognise the importance of social and economic factors, which lay outside the collective security mandate of the Security Council. He had already argued in 1944 that 'the Assembly should be given functions which will enable it to be in practice the central body of the World Organisation with the World Council as the executive agency but not the controlling body'.[55]

As Harper and Sissons point out, given Evatt's previous warning of 'the danger of great power predominance ... [his] championing of the Assembly, in which the smaller powers were all represented, was the logical consequence'.[56] Harper and Sissons say that: 'It is evident from the record that Australia was one of the many countries supporting the enlargement of the Assembly's powers. It is equally evident that leadership in this struggle fell to Dr Evatt'.[57] Evatt circulated an amendment at San Francisco which would give the General Assembly the right to consider and recommend on 'any matter affecting international relations'.[58] When the great powers rejected the right of the General Assembly to discuss anything within the scope of 'international relations', Evatt responded by changing the wording — to give the General Assembly the right to discuss anything within the scope of the United Nations Charter. The amendment as ultimately passed gave the General Assembly the power to discuss anything within the scope of the Charter or 'relating to the powers and functions of its organs' except when the Security Council was actively considering a specific matter.[59] Lee claims with justification that this

was Evatt's greatest victory. The great powers had brought to San Francisco a design for a General Assembly with severely limited powers. Evatt persuaded them to accept the Australian Labor government's approach and to agree to an Assembly with powers as comprehensive as those listed in the United Nations Charter.[60]

As Harper and Sissons note, this 'put beyond dispute the Assembly's right fully to discuss and to make recommendations on two subjects for which Australia at the time considered international co-operation and General Assembly recommendations to be essential: dependent peoples and full employment'. The 'subsequent shift in the balance of power between the Security Council and the General Assembly has largely vindicated his stand at San Francisco'.[61]

In later years, Evatt would continue to urge the General Assembly to become involved where the Security Council was unwilling or unable to act.[62] Later, in 1949, Evatt would tell the Australian parliament that the outcome of the stalemate in the Security Council as the result of excessive use of the veto was that the General Assembly had a role far more important than that which was visualised at San Francisco ... There is no power in the Assembly so great that it does not attend to the opinion of the majority of the Assembly and the criticism publicly uttered in the Assembly. Equally there is no power so small that it cannot influence the decisions of the Assembly ... The fact is that the organisation is working. Make no mistake about that. It is there to stay.[63]

Contested topics

Those at the formation of this new international organisation had to grapple with a thorny question: how much sovereignty was any nation to surrender in exchange for the expectation of protection and security from other sovereign states?[64] In the legal terms used at the San Francisco Conference, this was the question of 'domestic jurisdiction'. Which acts would be dealt with by nations' own laws, without any other interference, and which would fall under the United Nations' aegis? Australia, and Evatt, played a significant role in the framing of this question and its partial answer.

The Dumbarton Oaks proposals would have enabled the Security Council to deal, using its full power, with any matter 'out of which a threat to the peace or breach of the peace or act of aggression had arisen', even though the matter might be purely within a country's borders. This would have instituted a Security Council dominated by great powers able to veto any action against themselves, while at the same time, acting in concert, they could ignore the principle of domestic jurisdiction when they wished to intervene in the internal affairs of a smaller country. Evatt cabled home from San Francisco on 18 May 1945:

We regard it as essential that the exclusion of matters of domestic jurisdiction should apply to decisions of the Security Council ... Without such a provision it would be possible for an Asiatic Power to object to our Migration Policy and if it could be shown that a threat to peace had arisen the Security Council could proceed to recommend a settlement involving change in our Migration Policy as a condition necessary to remove the threat to peace. We have been negotiating with the United Kingdom on this matter and hope that an acceptable redrafting of the Big Four

Proposal can be obtained. This is a matter of fundamental principle and we cannot compromise on it.[65]

He emphasised this again on 6 June 1945:

The vital importance of this matter for Australia needs no emphasis. Under the charter as thus interpreted migration policy would become subject to the power of the Security Council immediately any aggressor threatened to use force to extort concessions. It would be impossible for Australia to ratify a charter that contained such provisions.[66]

Evatt's fear — and not Evatt's alone — was that another country might threaten force against Australia to loosen or abandon its White Australia immigration policy.[67] A racially exclusionary immigration policy that had bipartisan support for most of the 20th century, the White Australia policy was originally introduced by the Labor Party. It was a policy considered important and valuable by many Labor Party members, politicians and trade unionists, and remained part of the ALP Platform until 1965.[68] It had bipartisan and popular support and no government, even if inclined, could have survived the popular disapproval of abandonment of these principles in the 1940s.[69] It combined protectionism — protecting white Australian workers' good wages and conditions from competition by non-union foreign workers — with racism.

Australia was not the only country to object to the possibility of immigration policies being subject to international intervention: so too did the United States, and other countries had other objections to their domestic sovereignty being infringed upon.[70] Indeed, the possibility of including some proposals for the protection of minorities in the League of Nations Covenant had been dropped because of their implication for the immigration policies of the United States and other countries.[71]

Evatt and his supporters forced a protective caveat: that nothing else in the Charter would permit the United Nations to interfere in matters 'essentially within the domestic jurisdiction' of any state.[72] The interpretation of this clause continues to be a vexed question, and one on which Evatt and Australian representatives would come to take varying positions depending on the specifics of the case.[73] For example, when the question of the continued existence of the fascist Franco regime was brought to the Security Council in 1946, Evatt argued that it was a matter of international jurisdiction.[74] Buckley et al generously propose that the

suggestion that Evatt was inconsistent over the question of domestic jurisdiction overlooks the fact that Evatt made a distinction between those nations that had fought the Axis and those that had not. The former had fought global Fascism and Evatt was determined that the UN and the peace settlements would rid the world of that evil.[75]

But Harper and Sissons contend:

Reviewing the policy of the Australian Labor government generally on the matter of domestic jurisdiction, it is difficult to find a basic consistency ... The Australian delegates tended at times to give varying and elastic definitions of domestic jurisdiction which caused confusion as to Australia's basic attitude.[76]

The domestic jurisdiction provision has subsequently been interpreted broadly to mean that when violations of human rights are 'flagrant', then they have 'international repercussions' and fall under United Nations' jurisdiction.[77] Evatt showed considerable energy in pursuing the goal of protecting Australia's right to make decisions about domestic policy, especially immigration policy, free of 'interference' by other nations. However, when it came to specific cases involving other nations, he was more willing to justify the extension of the United Nations' authority.[78]

The question of what was called 'trusteeship' was another instance in which Evatt's protection of Australia's interests conflicted with his position on how other nations' conduct should be policed. The concept of 'trusteeship' was a way for colonial nations to seek to combine new ideals of human rights and equity with their status as colonial possessors. Like the rest of the United Nations Charter, those aspects that dealt with colonial dependencies were a compromise: in this case, a compromise between 'powers seeking to conserve their jurisdiction over dependent territories and powers seeking to open dependent territories to international activity designed ultimately to lessen or terminate their dependence'.[79] The idea was that these nations were in the position of guardians of their colonies and colonial peoples. The sticking point was the right or otherwise of the United Nations to supervise the carrying out of the principles and polices determined for development and decolonisation.

The League of Nations Covenant had included an agreement that colonies and territories ought to be administered to promote their well-being and development. The United Nations Charter went further, calling for the promotion of 'progressive development towards self-government or independence'.[80] Indeed, the very first article of the Charter holds that the purpose of the United Nations is to 'develop friendly relations among nations, based on respect for the principle of equal rights and self-determination of peoples'.[81] The fact that the Trusteeship Council dissolved in 1994 with the independence of the last colonial possessions demonstrates that this commitment was genuine.

Evatt would declare: 'The Australian Delegation was the first to propose that the Charter should contain a declaration of the principle of trusteeship, i.e. that the main purpose of administration is the welfare and advancement of the peoples of dependent territories'.[82] Evatt's strong stand on trusteeship was not simply the product of his own opinions, but Australian government policy. Indeed, in June 1945 Chifley cabled to Evatt and Forde expressing appreciation for 'the way in which you have maintained principles of Australian policy under great difficulties' with regard to the trusteeship negotiations.[83]

Certainly, Australia and New Zealand took a different position from the United Kingdom at the British Commonwealth meeting in April 1945.[84] Britain leaned towards the idea that colonial powers ought to be answerable to their own conscience rather than a third party or international committee, a position with which Australia disagreed.[85] With what Harper and Sissons describe as 'a strong socialist distrust of European imperialism combined with an awareness of the nationalist aspirations of colonial peoples', Australia felt that the principles of trusteeship should be extended to all colonies whether or not they were held as mandates, with an expert United Nations commission exercising supervision over administration.[86] Australia was, however, determined to exercise full control over its own trust territory of New Guinea and remained sensitive to criticism and interference in the South Pacific.[87]

The Charter

The San Francisco Conference achieved a mammoth task. In two months, the United Nations moved from draft to reality; two months in which every aspect of the Charter was examined and many changes were made.[88] The United Nations formally came into existence on 24 October 1945, upon the ratification of the Charter by the five permanent members of the Security Council and a majority of the other signatories. Writing in 1995, 50 years after the San Francisco Conference, Roberts and Kingsbury declared that the 'centre-piece of the UN's proclamation of international principles and standards remains even today the Charter of 1945'.[89]

The United Nations Charter is a product of idealism and pragmatism combined. As Roberts and Kingsbury wrote, 'it is extremely cautious in what it says about disarmament; and it refers not to the long-asserted but highly problematic principle of "national self-determination", but to the much vaguer formulation "equal rights and self-determination of peoples", which was less haunted by ghosts from Europe's history between the two world wars'.[90] Rosemary Righter, critical of many aspects of the United Nations, still feels that the Charter is

a document of considerable moral resonance. It broke new ground: in the detail of its provisions for the collective use of force; in the explicit connectives it drew between peace and material well-being; and perhaps above all in its determination, through a global organisation, to encourage states to respect not only other states, but their own people ... That the Charter of the United Nations was all-embracing was its architects' special pride; that it confronted the real world of sovereign recalcitrance and power politics was their source of hope ... However contradictory and loosely connected its various structural elements, the United Nations created spaces for multilateral mediation that were, in the already dangerously tense circumstances of 1945, a considerable and necessary achievement.[91]

The Charter is not the achievement of one man or one nation, but Evatt and the Australian delegation had reason to be proud of the role they had played. As Lee wrote:

Evatt participated in the formulation of the Chapter in the Charter on trusteeship which formed the basis for the subsequent involvement of the United Nations Organisation in decolonisation. And he incorporated into the constitution of the United Nations amendments protecting the territorial integrity and political independence of states; amendments providing that peaceful settlement proceed 'not arbitrarily but in conformity with the principles of justice and international law'; and amendments to ensure that the election of members to the Security Council pay attention to proven ability to contribute to international security and to geographical representation.[92]

At the final meeting of the Steering Committee, the delegate from Peru proposed a motion 'to pay homage here to the small nations represented at the Conference and to their great champion, Dr Evatt', indicating, as Plant says, 'the prominence which Evatt had achieved for himself and his country through his membership of the Executive Committee and of the persistence and aggressive energy with which he had argued Australia's policies at San Francisco'.[93]

Evatt boasted in a cablegram to Chifley, Beasley and Makin on 24 June 1945, that the 'Steering Committee consisting of heads of all delegations gave me a special vote by acclamation acclaiming me as one who did most to help in making of Charter by gallant fighting on behalf of middle and small nations'.[94] Harper and Sissons point out that:

Australia filed thirty-eight distinct amendments of substance; of these, twenty-six were 'adopted without material change, adopted in principle or made unnecessary by other alterations'. It would be absurd to claim for Australia an exclusive or even a primary share in the adoption of specific proposals: some of them had been accepted before the Conference by the great powers, and others had been advanced in slightly different form by the delegations of the smaller powers. Yet the Australian initiative had been an important one both in the drafting process and in the organising of support for particular amendments: Dr Evatt's personal influence was very considerable.[95]

Harper and Sissons say these contributions ought to be placed in the context of 'a social democratic tradition and a quickening national consciousness and a national pride'.[96] Sumner Wells, former US Assistant Secretary of State, declared of Evatt on one occasion:

I know of no modern statesman who has been more constructive and more courageous in the fight which he has made for the establishment of a constructive and realistic basis of truly democratic principles to govern the relations between nations in the new world order to come.[97]

And on another:

Australia has made the most notable contribution ... to the creation of those precedents and to the establishment of those principles which alone can transform the present United Nations into a strong world order based on justice and international morality.[98]

And Edward Stettinius, the US delegate to the Security Council, said 'Dr Evatt has done more than any other person to write the United Nations Charter. His work at San Francisco gained the admiration and respect of all nations'.[99]

3. The UN in practice

Evatt's great achievement at the San Francisco Conference was not the end of his or the Australian government's dedication to the ideal or practice of the United Nations. The conclusive victory of the Chifley government in the 1946 elections was a vote by the people for 'a postwar society in which an interventionist federal government would play a large role in ensuring the economic security of all Australians'.[1] It also provided Evatt with another term as foreign minister to build on and consolidate his achievements at San Francisco.

Regardless of the remarkable successes of San Francisco, Evatt's hopes were tempered with realism. Some historians, such as Renouf, find a contradiction in Evatt's ongoing commitment to the United Nations despite the emergence of serious flaws.[2] Renouf argues that the failures of the United Nations and Evatt's continuing commitment to the organisation regardless are indicative of his failure to understand the realities of world politics.[3]

Evatt was a product of the Australian political scene and the Australian Labor Party — environments in which change is gradual rather than revolutionary, parliamentarianism maintains primacy and flawed institutions are better than none.[4] As Senator John Faulkner said in his John Curtin Anniversary Lecture in 2006, 'Labor is a party of reform that does not chafe against the limitations of democracy. Labor does not see reform as second best to revolution and that has always been our unique quality in the Australian political landscape'.[5] Geoffrey Sawer wrote in 1956 that Evatt 'hoped for and believed in the UN whereas his conservative successors as Minister for External Affairs ... only hoped'.[6] Buckley et al note that despite Evatt's 'active role on the UN he was aware of its limitations from the beginning ... Having failed to eliminate ... [the Security Council] veto at San Francisco he warned of acute "pessimism" in world affairs and counselled against the "risks of a big power peace"'.[7]

Waters argues that under Prime Minister Ben Chifley, after John Curtin's death, the Labor government remained oriented to a new world order, based on 'the understanding that the foundations for long-term peace were economic prosperity and improving social conditions, and the belief that secret diplomacy, alliance diplomacy, and the development of strategic power leads to war'.[8] Waters goes on:

Accordingly, the solutions to international conflict which the Chifley government followed included policies directed to economic growth and achieving full employment, policies directed to meeting the fundamental political, economic and social needs of people, the use of multilateral institutions and diplomatic initiatives to resolve international conflict, the international control of the supply of arms to trouble spots, the universal application of human rights to all men and women, self-determination for all peoples leading to the end of colonialism, and the application of the rule of law to international relations.[9]

The Labor government was sharply aware of Australia's position as a small nation recently threatened by possible invasion. The commitment to the United Nations was integral to the Chifley government's security policy, with the aim of increasing Australia's influence and creating an international environment in which the country's interests were protected by principles of law and justice.[10]

Evatt's position at the Paris Peace Conference in 1946 was consistent with the position he had taken at San Francisco — resistance to domination by the great powers, argument for working processes rather than rubber stamps, and emphasis on political and economic rights.[11] Waters gives an evocative description of Evatt at the opening of the Paris Conference:

a solid figure of a man in an untidy suit rose from his seat ... challenging the rules of procedure suggested by the Foreign Ministers of the four great powers. He made a strong plea for the conference to adopt democratic procedures and for the right of the smaller belligerents to have a full part in drawing up the peace treaties … The man whose intervention the *Sydney Morning Herald* reported as having 'turned the proceedings in a couple of minutes from a dignified ceremonial into a real event' was … Evatt.[12]

Evatt assiduously collected complimentary press reports, including one from the French newspaper *Populaire* saying that, as he spoke, 'one hears the voice of the people'. And another: 'There is at this (Paris) Conference a man whom the French would like to be able to claim as a Frenchman. He plays in the name of his country a role which one would have wished to see our country play — that of the champion of small powers, of liberty, and of the rights of man'.[13] Subsequently, between 1946 and 1948, Buckley et al say:

Evatt earned the reputation of being one who would not hesitate to use the UN to conciliate conflict between the rivals in the Cold War. To the consternation of the Americans and the British, he seemed not to take sides. Evatt wanted the UN in Iran, for example, to conduct a thorough investigation which would include the 'reasons behind the Soviet refusal to withdraw troops'. The issue was not, in Evatt's view, just a dispute between the Soviets and Iran, as Britain and the United States had seen it. Similarly, during the Berlin blockade, imposed by the Soviet Union after Western allies announced the economic integration of their occupation zones into the state of West Germany, Evatt appealed for reconciliation. In Korea he did not go along with the American attempt to sponsor elections only in their zone of occupation in the south of the country. On no occasion, he argued, had the UN been given evidence to suggest that the Korean dispute could not be resolved nationally. To Evatt it was a question of due process … In these cases Evatt pointed out the wisdom of his position taken since the San Francisco Conference — that in the event that the Big Powers fell out and resorted to the use of the veto in the Security Council, the General Assembly must ensure that the issues could be openly investigated and debated. Providing that this procedure was not abused, Evatt assumed that the merits of each case could be assessed and the organisation could then take the appropriate action.[14]

'Privileging the position of the great powers', writes Waters, 'was a policy consistently opposed by the Australian Labor governments of the 1940s, as was the general approach to international relations of using power politics'.[15]

Evatt continued to play a very active part in Australia's work in the United Nations, but Renouf argues:

his work never again reached the very high standard it had at UNCIO. The qualities required were different. At San Francisco, Evatt's expertise in constitution-making and procedures was invaluable, and he was able to cloak his nationalism with internationalism. Thereafter, what was needed more was a capacity to find, with others, solutions of specific and complicated problems into which Australia's interests frequently and obviously intruded.[16]

Between the San Francisco Conference and the defeat of the Chifley government in 1949, the United Nations framework set out in 1945 was tested in practice — tests which Evatt was determined to see the fledgling organisation pass, but which would prove even tougher than the challenges of San Francisco.

Australia and the Security Council

The Chifley government maintained an emphasis on the United Nations in foreign policy, fighting for and winning a position as a founding non-permanent member of the Security Council in 1946 — providing an ongoing platform for Evatt to press for Australia's international program and priorities.[17] Australia and Canada tied for the position, and Canada withdrew.[18] Many of the smaller and medium powers with which Evatt had worked closely at the UNCIO supported Australia's election, which he believed had enabled Australia to defeat the 'ticket' more agreeable to the 'great powers'.[19] Among the congratulatory telegrams Evatt received was one from Manuel Eduardo Hunter, *chargé d'affaires en titre* of the Republic of Chile, declaring extravagantly that the 'seat obtained by Australia in Security Council of UNO means a victory for the democratic spirit of the New World and the most brilliant culmination of your untiring efforts at the San Francisco Conference'.[20]

Waters draws a parallel between Evatt's vigorous fight for membership of the Security Council and Evatt's drive to become President of the General Assembly in 1948, arguing that if

it had been ambition alone that drove Evatt, having achieved the office, he would have acted in the interests of the western powers and been showered with honours. But rather he chose the unpopular, more politically difficult course of independent conciliation. What Evatt and Burton were trying to achieve was a new order of international relations in which conflict was resolved not by power but by the rule of law ... an international order in which Australia's influence and power would be maximised.[21]

The failure to reach satisfactory solutions at the first meetings of the Security Council, while confirming Evatt in his stand on the veto, did not weaken his faith in the United Nations. 'Not all the issues brought before the Security Council have been finally settled. But the methods used in the effort to conciliate them have been those of frank public discussion and not those of secret diplomacy and open power politics'.[22] Indeed, 'Evatt believed that the Security Council was a quasi-judicial body which should play the same part in non-justiciable disputes as the International Court of Justice played in justiciable ones', acting 'in conformity with the principles of justice and international law'.[23]

The possibility of Security Council action against Spain in April 1946 and against Czechoslovakia in 1948 was foiled by the Soviet Union's use of the veto.[24] It was becoming clear, to Evatt and others, that potential Security Council action would be consistently blocked by the use of the veto in pursuit of Cold War ends. The problem became the subject of debate in the General Assembly and Evatt and his advisers would later report:

Australia took the lead in these debates [on voting procedures in the Security Council and the veto] ... at an early state in the debate it became evident that our dissatisfaction regarding the way in which the voting procedures under Article 27 had been applied in the Security Council during the past year was shared by a large majority of the members, and there was a wide measure of agreement that some urgent steps should be taken to ensure that the power of veto was not used in a way which would stultify the Council and prevent it from discharging its functions in respect to the maintenance of international peace and security. [25]

The Security Council did not live up to Evatt's hopes. Mired in veto deadlock, stymied by power politics, it could not be steered towards a useful role by all Evatt's proceduralism. His anxiety about the veto had proved prescient.[26] So, too, did his hopes that the General Assembly's rights and powers would enable this more democratic body to play a more useful role.

The UN Atomic Energy Commission

The 'scourge of war' had a new and sharper edge of anxiety after Hiroshima and Nagasaki. The years of 'Mutually Assured Destruction' still lay in the future, with the Cold War. In 1945, one country — the United States — had the bomb. The United Nations moved to put the genie back in the bottle.

In 1946 the General Assembly set up the Atomic Energy Commission (AEC or UNAEC). Evatt, carrying out the Chifley government's policy, supported this initiative.[27] Lee describes the Australian policy as support for 'a system whereby the AEC would own the plants producing atomic fuel, have a monopoly over research for the development of atomic weapons, and have uninhibited power to inspect the scientific and industrial establishments of individual states'.[28] As Buckley et al describe, from the beginning the UNAEC was bedevilled by the competing interests of nations reluctant to surrender or forgo possible military advantage. By June 1946, with the presentation of the Lilienthal and Baruch reports to the United Nations by the United States, it was clear that America envisioned control of 'peaceful' atomic power and raw materials but would not dismantle its stockpile of bombs until a system of controls was established. Evatt 'was, however, under no illusions as to the purposes behind the plans. The Lilienthal Report, he advised the

Department of External Affairs on 30 May 1946, was designed to "protect the United States from atom bomb attack. It preserves her supremacy in atomic armament and scientific application for a considerable period"'.[29]

When the UNAEC first met in June, the United States proposed a new body, an International Atomic Energy Authority, which would supervise the production of atomic energy once a control system had been created, with existing atomic bombs to be destroyed and no new bombs to be manufactured. The Soviet Union's counterproposal was an international convention to outlaw atomic bombs. When the United States proposals met wider approval, the Soviets argued that control of atomic bombs should be in the hands of the Security Council, with the permanent members' veto to apply as in any other decision.[30]

These counterproposals have been characterised by historians such as Amos Yoder as political posturing with no expectation of success.[31] Evatt endeavoured to find a middle ground, arguing:

Past experience of international pacts suggests that mere undertakings by nations to cease production of atomic weapons, to destroy existing stocks and not to use atomic weapons for purposes of war would not be sufficient; if so, such undertakings should be linked to and integrated with positive and continuous measures of control. Such a system of control measures could not be made effective unless there is established some form of international agency. There cannot be inspections without inspectors, vested with the necessary powers. Such inspectors must be appointed by and responsible to some international agency ... Much of the work of an atomic energy agency would be concerned with such matters as inspection, licensing, collection and dissemination of statistics, research and development. Such matters are quite distinct from the very special kind of dispute or situation over which the Security Council is given jurisdiction by the United Nations Charter. [32]

Evatt therefore argued for a new organisation.[33] This organisation was not instituted during Evatt's time on the UNAEC. In 1949, to Evatt's disappointment, the UNAEC decided to adjourn indefinitely.[34] The UNAEC did not succeed in establishing effective international control over nuclear weapons. The nuclear threat would hang over the world for decades to come.

Palestine and Israel

International horror at the atrocities of the Holocaust strengthened the cause of the Zionist movement seeking to establish a Jewish homeland in Palestine. This proposal was resisted by many Palestinians, at times violently. Britain, made responsible for Palestine by the League of Nations after World War I, tried to contain the situation by limiting Jewish migration to Palestine. The policy was unpopular, domestically and internationally, and in April 1947 Britain asked for the question of Palestine to be placed on the agenda of a regular session of the General Assembly.[35]

For Evatt, the question of Palestine had a greater significance. This submission to the United Nations of a problem insoluble by domestic means was simultaneously a vote of confidence in the fledgling international organisation and an opportunity for public and spectacular failure.[36] Historians agree Evatt played a crucial role.[37] It was the Australian delegation which successfully moved in the General Assembly in May 1947 the resolution 'to establish a committee of enquiry to investigate the issue. The United Nations Special Committee on Palestine (UNSCOP) ... would be made up exclusively of smaller 'neutral' powers — including Australia'.[38]

Perhaps unsurprisingly, in September UNSCOP failed to produce a united report. The majority report recommended partition into two independent states, Arab and Jewish. The minority report supported a single state. Australia supported neither solution.[39] A further committee, chaired by Evatt, divided into three subcommittees: 'Committee 1 dealt with the Majority Report of UNSCOP which had favoured partition, while Committee 2 dealt with the Minority Report which favoured a unitary state. Evatt himself headed a third committee that would attempt to reconcile opposing views, a measure that in any case followed seventeen meetings of the Ad Hoc Committee that made it clear there was no common ground'.[40] Evatt later wrote: 'In the ad hoc committee I struggled for two months so that the delegates would finally face up to the issues on the vote'.[41] Evatt came out for partition.[42]

The General Assembly voted for partition on 9 November 1947.[43] When fighting broke out, the Americans and British had second thoughts about the solution.[44] Evatt wrote to the Secretary General, Trygve Lie:

The position with regard to Palestine is in my judgement the most critical in the history of the United Nations. The choice now is between a complete washout and a positive solution. In such a situation abstention can only mean a direct invitation to the two groups in Palestine to fight it out on the battlefield with the United Nations, which is supposed to maintain peace, not even offering a just solution … Indeed it would reduce the high status of the assembly to the discredited status now occupied by the security council.[45]

Evatt sprang to the defence of the new state. Buckley et al write that Evatt

argued, successfully, that the United Nations was obliged to take enforcement action 'irrespective of the status of Israel' since a threat to peace had occurred. He attacked the attempt to reduce the new state … He also sought to have Israel admitted to the United Nations — a move that would overcome concern about its 'status' and which would allow the fledgling state to arm itself. Only on the question of the internationalisation of Jerusalem did Evatt disappoint the Israelis when they demanded sovereign control of the city.[46]

In the 1948 report on the work of the Australian delegation to the General Assembly, the country's role in the Palestinian decision was a source of pride:

Australia has always maintained that the decisions of the United Nations must be supported and upheld. The 1947 Assembly declaration of

Palestine was adopted after long and careful study, in the course of which the views of all interested parties were heard and examined … Australia has therefore introduced in the Assembly a resolution on Palestine which takes the Assembly's decision of November 1947 as the basis for subsequent United Nations action; accepts the existence of Israel as a properly and effectively established State; and seeks to secure a permanent settlement between Israel and the Arabs on the basis of agreement between them, reached with the assistance of conciliation machinery of the United Nations. This approach realistically accepts the facts of the situation in the Middle East and points a way to a just solution.[47]

In 1948 Evatt told the Australian Institute of Political Science Winter Forum that the United Nations had failed to solve the Palestine question — due not to 'the weakness of the Charter of the United Nations, nor to the type of decision reached by the General Assembly [but to] the failure of the Member Governments of the United Nations to abide by the obligations which they themselves have undertaken by having become members of the United Nations itself'.[48] But by 1949 Evatt wrote, '[t]here is now a real basis for hope that the Arabs and Jews can live together in peace in this important region'.[49] Such optimism was misplaced.

1. Independent foreign policy. Evatt with the leader of the UK delegation, Anthony Eden. San Francisco Conference, 5 May 1945.

2. Pre-Cold War order. UNCIO executive committee in session, 8 May 1945. Evatt is seated fifth from the left, between the Prime Minister of Canada, McKenzie King, and the UK leader, Anthony Eden. The other members present were from China, US (Chair, Edward Stettinius, assisted by Alger Hiss), USSR (V. M. Molotov), Czechoslovakia, Yugoslavia, Netherlands, Iran and France. OWI staff photo.

Left **3. A woman looks on.** Voting at a meeting of Committee 1, San Francisco Conference, 12 June 1945.

Above **4. Flags and badges.** Evatt signing the Charter of the United Nations at the San Francisco Conference, 26 June 1945. Delegates from 50 nations met between 25 April and 26 June. The Charter was adopted unanimously on 24 October 1945. This picture was taken at the San Francisco War Memorial Opera House.

5. In the open daylight.
H. V. Evatt and Mary Alice
Evatt leaving
the San Francisco
Conference, 1945.

6. President of the world.
Evatt was President of
the General Assembly
from September 1948 to
August 1949. The Universal
Declaration of Human
Rights was proclaimed on
10 December 1948. United
Nations Photo (Department
of Public Information)
UN 21845.

4. Human rights

The United Nations was based on the League of Nations. The first sentences of the preamble to both the League of Nations Covenant and the United Nations Charter express similar commitments to preventing war and respecting international law. The UN Charter also declares that the organisation is determined 'to reaffirm faith in fundamental human rights'.[1] This was the key difference between the League and the United Nations.[2]

Tony Evans has written that the 'creation of the United Nations placed universal human rights at the centre of global politics. Human rights are mentioned in the UN Charter seven times'.[3] Tom Farer and Felice Gaer argue that '[a]t its inception, the United Nations seemed destined to be the engine of human rights', but John P. Humphrey points out '[t]hat the human rights provisions of the charter, as finally adopted, are considerably stronger than those of the Dumbarton Oaks proposals, [which] was due largely to the efforts of the delegations of certain small countries at San Francisco'.[4]

Evatt went to San Francisco with the belief that peace, lasting peace, could not be secured without justice — justice that included but went beyond legalistic interpretations to include economic and social justice. He came up against two barriers — the barriers of power politics, soon to take a new form in the Cold War, and the barrier of a narrower conception of the role and function of the United Nations. Despite these obstacles, Evatt won significant victories. The triumph was not his or Australia's alone, but the skilful way in which Evatt negotiated with different interest groups at the San Francisco Conference enabled him to win concessions from the great powers. Evatt wrote later that Australia 'did not belong to any bloc of nations'.[5] The Australian delegation joined forces with the small and medium powers at the UNCIO to argue for extending the powers of the General Assembly with the Soviet Union their significant opponent, but then combined with the Soviet Union and other countries of what would become the Eastern Bloc to press through the pledge on full employment.[6]

As I have argued, the procedural reforms discussed above were an end in themselves for Evatt, in his determination to make the United Nations a functioning and democratic organisation. But they were also a necessary precondition for the changes Evatt envisaged to the scope and functions of the United Nations. The international security agenda of the Curtin and Chifley governments, shaped and implemented by Doc Evatt, was broader than the narrow conception of the St James Palace Declaration or the Dumbarton Oaks proposals. Evatt, and Labor, believed that international security depended heavily on people having economic security and political freedoms. As we have seen, this agenda was expressed at the San Francisco Conference, at the Paris Peace Conference, and many times domestically in Australia by Evatt and other members of the Curtin government.

Consequently, as Harper and Sissons note, 'one of the most strenuously pursued objectives of Australia was the conversion of the social and economic chapters of the Dumbarton Oaks drafts from a "frigid" into a "full-blooded" document'.[7] Buckley et al describe Evatt 'outflanking' the great powers at the UNCIO

by stressing that international peace was not simply secured by security measures, it also needed 'positive' measures ... Organisations such as the United Nations Relief and Rehabilitation Administration (UNRRA) and the Food and Agriculture Organisation (FAO), in Evatt's view, had to be adequately supported by the world community to tackle the root causes of war — social and economic insecurity.[8]

Lee describes the foreign economic policy of the Labor governments of the 1940s as being 'to mould the US doctrine of multilateralism into a regime which maintained full employment and encouraged development in the Third World'. For example, it 'was the Labor government which laid the foundations for the aid program to Southeast Asia which subsequently became known as the Colombo Plan'.[9] Harper and Sissons characterise Australian foreign policy in this period as pursuing security through economic as well as military means, with the United Nations as an avenue.[10]

Lee credits Evatt with helping to extend the power and range of the United Nations Economic and Social Council.[11] The majority of delegates to the UNCIO resisted the idea that the United Nations ought to be able to take action to force members to observe human rights. A Panamanian proposal to include the protection as well as the promotion of human rights was rejected. The Australian delegation proposed a more moderate amendment — empowering the Economic and Social Council to promote observance of as well as respect for human rights, and this was more successful.[12]

One key item on Evatt's San Francisco agenda was a commitment to full employment. Evatt had been deeply affected by the misery and suffering in his neighbourhood of Balmain during the Great Depression.[13] The provision of work for all was a central tenet for the Labor Party of the 1940s. The Curtin and Chifley governments regarded employment as a prerequisite to enjoying other human rights and freedoms.[14] The Curtin government had begun endeavouring to involve wartime allies in the fight against unemployment during the war — at the Food and Agriculture Conference in 1943 and at the International Labor Organisation conference in 1944.[15] The Australian efforts to introduce full employment into the charter are part of that continuum and were successful despite American preference for the less absolute phrase 'high and continuing levels of employment'.[16]

Lee credits the international commitment to full employment and higher standards of living in the UN Charter to Evatt's efforts and argues that this struggle 'was consistent with the Curtin government's new international economic policies'.[17] Evatt cabled home triumphantly:

I am sure that you will be delighted to hear that Conference has not only agreed to full employment as an objective but will include in charter a pledge by each nation to pursue that objective internally as well as by international action. Australia's work at Hot Springs, Bretton Woods and Philadelphia has been vindicated and our policy of four years has been adopted. The result will be written not in a temporary agreement but in the Charter solemnly signed by all United Nations.[18]

Economic security through employment was part of the 'social and economic' side of human rights. At San Francisco, there were divergent opinions on the relative importance of social and economic rights versus political and civil rights. Evatt's position that political and civil rights were of equal importance — neither greater nor lesser — to economic and social rights places him and Australia between free market America and the communist Soviet bloc.[19] Labor has always held that civil rights cannot be exercised in economic bondage; economic rights cannot be secured without civil liberties.[20] Evatt's commitment to human rights was consistent with that view, and he used Australia's position as an independent middle power in an effort to move opinion at the United Nations towards that objective.

The first session of the Economic and Social Council in January and February 1946 established a Commission on Human Rights, as called for in the UN Charter.[21] By the time the first regular session of the Commission opened in January 1947, the emerging divisions of the coming Cold War had raised tensions. Chaired by Eleanor Roosevelt, the 'first regular session of the Commission opened on 27 January 1947, in an atmosphere of increasing East-West tension'.[22] Initially the task of drafting the International Bill of Rights was referred to the Commission's bureau, but

the Soviet delegation at the next session of the Economic and Social Council, which met in March, attacked the Commission's decision on the ground that the drafting committee was not representative — which indeed it was not — and Mrs Roosevelt ... created a new drafting committee, consisting of the members of the Commission representing Australia, Chile, China, the United States, France, Lebanon, the United Kingdom and the USSR.[23]

Garry Woodard suggests that though John P. Humphrey in the UN Secretariat did the bulk of the drafting work for the committee, he 'was able to use Australia's earlier efforts to include in his first draft full coverage of economic and social rights'. Woodard describes Australia's role in the drafting as 'an honourable but not leading one'.[24] Evatt maintained close contact with Australia's representatives at the United Nations in this period, including constant encouragement to pursue the Australian policy objectives laid out at the San Francisco Conference.[25]

For Evatt, 1948 was a momentous year. That year he was elected President of the General Assembly of the United Nations. Although in the 21st century the President of the General Assembly often seems to be a role with less public presence and less significance than the Secretary-General, viewed in the context of Evatt's determination to expand the powers and role of the Assembly and emphasise the United Nations' role as a working democratic institution, the position of President, with its responsibility of Chairing the General Assembly, was a highly significant position.

At the opening of the General Assembly in Paris in 1948, the parade of arriving dignitaries was interrupted by

a modest, late-model Ford ... a heavy, tousle-headed man in a baggy lounge suit, his tie off-centre, sat next to the chauffeur. Muttering a nasal 'see you later' to the driver, the passenger let himself out and shambled up to the official entrance — only to be barred by a gendarme whose instructions were to admit dignitaries only. Later the policeman was flabbergasted to learn that he had delayed the President of the General Assembly himself, Dr Evatt.[26]

The report of the Australian delegation to the Third Session of the General Assembly says, with perhaps some hyperbole:

> The responsibilities and influence of Australia have been greatly increased in Paris by the election of Dr Evatt to the Presidency of the General Assembly. This is the highest position in international affairs ever attained by an Australian, and is a recognition both to himself and the policies which Australia has followed and advocated. As President, Dr Evatt has regarded himself as the representative of all the 58 nations comprising the Assembly and as the upholder and asserter of the Assembly's rights and duties.[27]

In a flattering tone, but one that reflects Evatt's own preoccupations and his belief in the potential of the United Nations, the report continued:

> Upon the President falls the duty of making the Assembly run smoothly and the transaction and guidance of its business. But he has an even greater task in giving leadership in the field of policy. Dr Evatt has worked unceasingly to make the present session a successful one — to ensure that the Assembly is not just a debating society, but a body working sincerely to find solutions to the problems coming before it.[28]

As President of the General Assembly, Evatt presided over the adoption on 10 December 1948 of the Universal Declaration of Human Rights (UDHR). Forty-eight nations voted in favour, eight abstained and two were absent. No nation voted against. Evatt considered the Universal Declaration as a crucial achievement of the United Nations. In a statement written for the Newspaper Enterprise Association (NEA) syndicated news service during his term as President, Evatt described 'tyranny and oppression' as one of the three great enemies of mankind and said: 'Much detailed work has been done in this field by the United Nations. These efforts, I hope, will be crowned in this third session of the General Assembly by the adoption of a Declaration of Human Rights, and of a convention for the prevention and punishment of genocide'.[29]

The report of the Australian delegation to the Third Session of the General Assembly states:

The Declaration will have great moral force as a standard, and helps to explain the general references to human rights contained in the United Nations Charter. At the same time, the Australian delegation has stated that a covenant and measures of carrying out and enforcing rights should be completed as soon as possible … Australia has from the beginning been one of the leaders in this field. We urged at the Paris Peace Conference that the peace treaties with enemy states should contain effective guarantees of human rights. We have also played our part from the beginning as a member of the United Nations Commission on Human Rights which made the first draft of the convention. Australia was one of the first countries to urge that economic and social rights should be included in the Declaration … Final adoption of the Declaration has been slow work. The Declaration covers a very wide field, including rights of personal liberty, political rights, and economic and social rights. It flows from the legal systems of 58 nations. The Australian delegation has worked successfully to keep each article clear and concise, expressing the broad, fundamental human rights. It has resisted attempts to write in a series of limitations which should properly be done in the legally-binding convention.[30]

Evatt said:

It was the first occasion on which the organised community of nations had made a declaration of human rights and fundamental freedoms. That document was backed by the authority of the body of opinion of the United Nations as a whole and millions of people, men, women, and children all over the world, would turn to it for help, guidance and inspiration.[31]

After the adoption of the UDHR, the commission immediately began work on two covenants incorporating the principles of the declaration: one on civil and political rights, and one on economic and cultural rights.[32] Those covenants would not be complete until 1966, the year after Evatt's death, but inasmuch as they carried out the principles of the UDHR, over which he had exerted significant influence through both his work on the Charter and Australia's role in the drafting, the covenants can also be said to be in some ways an outcome of his work.

The UDHR is not an uncontroversial document. Evan Luard argues that much of the declaration consists of 'well-meaning platitudes that any government on earth could happily assent to without altering its existing policies one iota'.[33] But, as Luard continues: 'The more specific a clause is, the more likely it is that some governments will wish to dissent from it. Imprecision is often the price of unanimity'.[34] A less kindly view is that of Rosemary Righter. She writes:

The constitutions of the UN and the specialised agencies are fine expressions of liberal ideals and benign purposes centred on individual rights ... But the guardianship of these rights ... has been assigned to governments — which lead the way in violating them. This paradox [is] inherent in the UN's structure.[35]

The Universal Declaration of Human Rights starts with the ringing declaration:

Whereas recognition of the inherent dignity and of the equal and inalienable rights of all members of the human family is the foundation of freedom, justice and peace in the world ... Whereas it is essential to promote the development of friendly relations between nations ... Now, therefore THE GENERAL ASSEMBLY proclaims THIS UNIVERSAL DECLARATION OF HUMAN RIGHTS as a common standard of achievement for all peoples.

It goes on to set out, in 30 Articles, a series of rights. While space precludes a complete discussion, some of the more notable statements include:

All human beings are born free and equal in dignity and rights ... Everyone is entitled to all the rights and freedoms set forth in this Declaration, without distinction of any kind ... Everyone has the right to life, liberty and security of person ... No one shall be held in slavery ... No one shall be subjected to torture or to cruel, inhuman or degrading treatment or punishment ... No one shall be subjected to arbitrary arrest, detention or exile ... Everyone is entitled in full equality to a fair and public hearing by an independent and impartial tribunal ... Everyone has the right to work, to free choice of employment, to just and favourable conditions of work and to protection against unemployment ... Everyone, without any discrimination, has the right to equal pay for equal work ... Everyone who works has the right to just and favourable remuneration ensuring for himself and his family an existence worthy of human dignity

... Everyone has the right to form and to join trade unions for the protection of his interests ... Everyone has the right to rest and leisure ... Everyone has the right to a standard of living adequate for the health and well-being of himself and of his family. [36]

The declaration has given rise to a comprehensive body of human rights law, which the United Nations claims 'for the first time in history, provides us with a universal and internationally protected code of human rights, one to which all nations can subscribe and to which all people can aspire'.[37] Tony Evans asserts that the Universal Declaration of Human Rights is central to legal discourse on human rights, and Ian Russell considered that it is 'often considered to have the weight of customary international law because it is so widely accepted'.[38]

While the original conception of the United Nations was of a body maintaining international security, now the protection of peace and personal safety is part of a greater framework of human rights protection. The framework guides almost all aspects of United Nations activity, often expressed in the vocabulary of comprehensive 'human security'. Evans cites the United Nations Development Program's definition of human security:

'safety from the constant threats of hunger, disease, crime and repression' and 'protection from sudden and hurtful disruptions to the patterns of our daily lives — whether in the home, in our jobs, in our community or in our environment'. Human security is not therefore only to do with cataclysmic political and international events, but with 'job security, income security, health security, environmental security ... [and] ... security from crime'.[39]

As Evans points out:

Human rights are mentioned in the UN Charter seven times, including Article 68, which calls for the creation of the Commission on Human Rights. The Commission completed the final draft of the Universal Declaration of Human Rights (UDHR) during its first eighteen months of deliberation, a remarkable achievement, rarely matched before or since, for reaching any international agreement. That the UDHR remains the single, most important statement of human rights norms, more than fifty years later, places this achievement into even sharper perspective.[40]

Humphrey also places the achievement of drafting and adopting the UDHR at the centre of the United Nations' achievements:

To anyone familiar with the United Nations, this was a remarkable achievement. Indeed, one of the best contemporary writers on international organisation has said that the adoption of the Declaration was probably 'the major achievement of the United Nations'. In less than two years, the organisation had been able to agree on the adoption of a text in a matter which was not only rife with difficulties but which went to the very heart of the ideological conflict which had bedevilled the United Nations ever since San Francisco and is still largely responsible for preventing the organisation from carrying out the major functions with which it is charged by the Charter.[41]

Humphrey goes on to say that

[e]ven more remarkable than the performance of the United Nations in adopting the Declaration has been its impact and the role which it almost immediately began to play both within and outside the United Nations — an impact and a role which probably exceed the most sanguine hopes of its authors. No other act of the United Nations has had anything like the same impact on the thinking of our time, the best aspirations of which it incorporates and proclaims. It may well be that it will live in history chiefly as a statement of great moral principles. As such its influence is deeper than any political document or legal instrument. Men of affairs, however, are more apt to be impressed by the political and legal authority which it has established for itself. Its political authority is now second only to that of the charter itself. Indeed its reception at all levels has been such that, contrary to the expressed intention of its authors, it may have now become part of international law.[42]

The Universal Declaration of Human Rights, and its impact, was the culmination of the work that Evatt and his advisers had been doing since the emergence of proposals for a new international organisation during World War II. It casts international security in the context of human rights — human rights conceived in the broadest sense. It was apt and fitting that Evatt, part of and key proponent for an Australian Labor policy tradition of liberal internationalism that saw the protection of human rights and human security as the key to the making 'of peace which all the peoples of the world desire', presided over the session of the General Assembly that adopted the statement.[43]

5. Legacy

Evatt's term as President of the General Assembly came at the end of his time as an active participant in the United Nations. His term concluded in September 1949 and in December 1949 the Chifley government was swept from office in an election marked by Cold War anxiety about communism.[1]

For Evatt, the change in fortune must have been marked. In 1949 he was President of the General Assembly of the United Nations. In 1950 he was an opposition member of parliament opening the United Nations Festival in Geelong, Victoria. The consistency of his dedication to the ideals he had pursued in office is clear in the words he wrote for the foreword to the official program of the Festival — the original preserved in the Evatt Collection, with Evatt's meticulous amendments showing his painstaking attention to a task many less distinguished politicians before and after his time would have regarded as beneath them. 'The road to peace is never easy, and it is sometimes dangerous' he wrote:

The world desperately needs people who will have the wisdom and the courage to travel that road, and to insist that their governments make no detours around it. [The United Nations'] long-range efforts ... seek to remove the causes of economic insecurity among peoples. They seek to improve the social conditions of peoples throughout the world. They attach great importance to human rights and fundamental freedoms ... The one world organisation in which these great objectives may be actively practised is in the United Nations. It is necessary to give it unfaltering and unwavering support.[2]

In the margin, Evatt added: 'International peace is not divisible'.

Evatt would never again be a federal minister. After Chifley's death in 1951, he became Federal Labor Leader. The struggle between the anti-communist Catholic 'Industrial Groups' and the left of the Labor Party increased in intensity during Evatt's leadership, and in 1955 a devastating split — devastating enough in the history of a party bedevilled by division to be described as 'The Split' — consigned the ALP to the electoral wilderness, where it would remain until Gough Whitlam's 1972 victory. Evatt's behaviour and personality became markedly more erratic. In 1960 he retired from politics to be appointed Chief Justice of the New South Wales Supreme Court, a position he held with a sad lack of distinction until he suffered a stroke in 1962, dying three years later.[3]

For many Australians, knowing Evatt primarily as a domestic political figure, his quixotic decisions to oppose Menzies' 1951 referendum to outlaw the Communist Party and to personally appear before the Petrov Inquiry to defend members of his staff accused of Soviet espionage, and his pugnacious and divisive behaviour in facing internal party conflicts, leave the impression of a reckless and combative figure, lacking political acumen.[4]

Whatever the accuracy of this characterisation of Evatt during the 1950s, in the eight years between 1941 and 1949, in which he was the principal architect and enactor of Australia's foreign policy, he left a legacy on the Australian political scene and the international arena that still endures. Renouf characterised Evatt's performance at the UNCIO as:

of virtuoso quality: for sheer brilliance in an international forum there is nothing in Australia's diplomatic annals to surpass it. For the public, he was one of the outstanding personalities (newspaper representatives voted Harold Stassen of the United States and Evatt as the most impressive delegates). Abroad, he was loaded with praise ... The reputation Evatt won for himself as the voice of Australia long endured in the United Nations. It brought great credit to his country; more than any other national leader, Evatt made Australia known universally and made it known as a country of courage, responsibility and liberalism ... Deprived throughout the war of the say to which Evatt thought Australia was entitled, he had his reward at San Francisco, where Australia was heard as never before. What was of more lasting value was that when it was heard, it had something worthwhile to say.[5]

Cornelia Meigs described him as:

the generally acknowledged leader of the whole strength of the Smaller Powers ... He had come armed and girded with relentless determination to see that the rights of the lesser nations did not disappear under the shadow of the greater ones. And he had won the respect of all — great countries as well as small ... His was real and brilliant statesmanship, resourceful, constructive. Yet he was no demagogue. He had the full weight of the smaller nations behind him, but he refrained from using their strength to block the proceedings of the Conference.[6]

Gareth Evans has said:

Dr Evatt's performance at San Francisco was the stuff of which legends are made – especially in his fights for the rights of the smaller powers against the greater in the roles of the General Assembly and the Security Council, and in his faith in the UN as an agent for social and economic reform and as a protector of human rights.[7]

That faith endured, even though

the nature of the post-war world turned out to be very different from what he had expected. He had hoped that the wartime collaboration of the Great Powers would go on; it did not. He had hoped that the smaller countries would act responsibly; many did not. An organisation of only fifty states had been created, and Evatt had thought that the membership would swell but slowly; it exploded. Evatt had considered that dependent peoples would be well satisfied with the new regime of the Charter; they asked for more, and the anti-colonial wave hit the United Nations. Evatt had felt that principle should have greater sway over international relations; events soon showed that little in this respect had changed. In brief, all the euphoria generated during the war and which reached a climax at UNCIO rapidly evaporated, and the United Nations became a disappointment.[8]

Renouf characterises Evatt as a prisoner of his own faith in the organisation he had helped create, writing that it

is curious that a man of Evatt's intelligence and experience had been unable to admit that, once formed, the UN had proved incapable of meeting the hopes that had been held of it ... He was unable to find any alternative except to persevere with the UN ... power politics, according to him, had to be controlled by world public opinion in support of law and order. For the purpose, there was no means other than the UN. Weak as it might be, one had to keep on supporting it, unwaveringly.[9]

There is an alternative explanation for Evatt's steadfast support for the United Nations and his efforts to persuade public opinion towards his own views. Evatt had by the early 1950s been pursuing reform in the interests of justice since his first days at the bar.[10] If he had started with the hope that success would be early and complete, it is hard to imagine such expectations enduring decades of setbacks and frustrations. Evatt's persistence was undaunted, even as he moved from state parliament to the High Court and then back to politics in the federal arena. His enduring faith in the potential of the United Nations, regardless of the visible flaws in the organisation's operation, can be seen in this light less as naïve than as the deliberate act of will of a man deciding that an imperfect institution is better than no institution at all; that it is better to seize the progress available and hope for more later than refuse any advances because they do not institute immediate Utopia. Indeed, he expressed a quintessentially Labor approach when he answered critics of the United Nations at the end of 1945 by saying that efforts to achieve an unobtainable world government or to utterly remove the veto would merely 'divert attention from the immediate task on hand: to work for the success of the United Nations Organisation which is already in existence'.[11]

Sixty-three years after its inception, opinion on the United Nations is *still* divided. The hopes of San Francisco have not been realised — but nor have the predictions of those who characterised the United Nations as a pointless exercise from the start. Roberts and Kingsbury point out that the body is too often evaluated against extravagantly high ideals — and perhaps the extravagantly high ideals set out in the Charter make such judgements inevitable.[12] Failing to meet the lofty claims of the Charter does not automatically mean the United Nations is a failure in itself. Roberts and Kingsbury point out that the United Nations' contribution has come to be seen by many as being less in the field of peace between the major powers than in other areas: defusing certain regional conflicts, advocating self-determination, assisting decolonisation, codifying international law, protecting human rights, and providing a possible framework for social economic improvement, even for redistribution of wealth on a global scale … The UN should be judged, not just by what it does in particular fields of activity, or in particular crises, but also by the way in which, through its very existence, through the influence of its Charter, through the questions it addresses, and through its diplomatic rituals, it proclaims certain values and sets the terms of international debates.[13]

In the *Australian Dictionary of Biography*, Geoffrey Bolton suggests that Evatt's work in the early years of the United Nations, by encouraging the organisation to develop as a genuine forum in which outcomes could not always be predicted by power politics or the emerging Cold War divisions, enhanced the United Nations' legitimacy and influence.[14]

In a statement written for the NEA syndicated news service during his term as President, Evatt declared that

to have stopped bloodshed and to have kept discussion going when deadlocks have been reached [are not small achievements] … in three years men and governments have been brought together in a common effort to fight poverty and other economic and social problems … in three years the United Nations has accomplished a great deal in fields of vital importance. It has done more than reasonable men expected in so short a period.[15]

In the same year, he told the Winter Forum of the Australian Institute of Political Science:

It is criminal that so soon after the conclusion of the last war people should already be talking of the next war, and actually accepting the inevitability of such a war. No war has ever been inevitable. The most certain way of ensuring that war will break out is to indulge in loose talk of war, to encourage power politics and to by-pass and misuse the machinery of international co-operation provided by the United Nations.[16]

Evatt's legacy to Australia and to the international community is in the institution he helped to found and in the breadth of the concerns within its mandate. But more, it is in his resolute optimism and determination to strive, even against absurd odds, to use his position and abilities to improve the world around him, and Australia's place in it.

The goals of the UN Charter, with its grand determination to rid the world 'of the scourge of war', may make cynics chuckle — but for Evatt and his colleagues, with two world wars and the devastation of the Great Depression in their lifetime, it was a real and earnest aim. As we are proud of the international efforts Evatt undertook in Australia's name, so too we ought to be spurred by those efforts to seek solutions to the same problems of war, poverty, injustice and inequality that were his life's work. 'This is a continuous task,' Evatt wrote in 1949. 'At no stage in the world's history will it be feasible to pause and assume that the task is finished'.[17] As the Doc wrote to conclude his summary of the United Nations' achievements, '[m]uch patient and hard work is necessary and always will be'.[18]

Endnotes

1 – Introduction

1 Ross McMullin, *The Light on the Hill: The Australian Labor Party 1891–1991* (Oxford University Press: Melbourne, 1991), pp. 270–87.

2 The most laudatory account of Evatt's actions is in Kylie Tennant, *Evatt: Politics and Justice* (Angus & Robertson: Sydney, 1970).

3 Evatt is most strongly characterised in this negative light by political opponents such as Howard Beale in *This Inch of Time: Memoirs of Politics and Diplomacy* and Paul Hasluck, *Diplomatic Witness,* both cited in P. G. Edwards, *Prime Ministers and Diplomats: The Making of Australian Foreign Policy 1901–1949* (Oxford University Press: Melbourne, 1983), pp. 141, 144.

4 McMullin, p. 245.

5 These events in Evatt's life are described in K. Buckley, B. Dale & W. Reynolds, *Doc Evatt* (Longman Cheshire: Melbourne, 1994), pp. 4–17; and in Tennant, pp. 5–30.

6 Buckley et al, pp. 16–44ff Alan Renouf, *Let Justice Be Done: The Foreign Policy of Dr H. V. Evatt* (University of Queensland Press: St Lucia, 1983), pp. 6ff. Tennant, pp. 23–55.

7 A detailed description of the internal Labor Party conflict in the NSW ALP can be found in Graham Freudenberg's *Cause for Power: The Official History of the New South Wales Branch of the Australian Labor Party* (Pluto Press: Sydney, 1991), pp. 148–52; these events in Evatt's life are described in Buckley et al, pp. 83–144.

8 David Day, *John Curtin: A Life* (Harper Collins: Sydney, 1999), pp. 342ff.

9 ibid., p. 384; Lloyd Ross, *John Curtin: A Biography* (Sun Papermac: Netley, SA 1983), pp. 206ff.

10 Day, pp. 411ff. Ross, pp. 207ff. Buckley et al., pp. 146ff; Terry Irving, 'The Growth of Federal Authority: 1929–1940' in John Faulkner & Stuart Macintyre (eds), *True Believers: The Story of the Federal Parliamentary Labor Party* (Allen & Unwin: Sydney, 2001), p. 74; a detailed discussion of the circumstances surrounding Labor's accession to power in 1941 can be found in Graham Freudenberg, 'Victory to Defeat: 1941–1949' in Faulkner & Macintyre, pp. 76–8; see also McMullin, pp. 205–7.

11 See, for example, Renouf, pp. 95–125.

12 McMullin, pp. 215–8; Day, pp. 448–59; Ross, pp. 260ff.

13 Buckley et al, pp. 153–4.

14 *Melbourne Herald,* 27 December 1941 (for Curtin's words). For Australia and the Commonwealth, see, for example, BBC Post-script Broadcast by the Rt Hon. H. V. Evatt, Minister for External Affairs, Commonwealth of Australia, 9.15 p.m., Sunday 27th June 1943 (Evatt Collection: Speeches and Statements): 'In the Pacific we fight not for ourselves alone but as trustees for the United Nations, particularly for the British Commonwealth of Nations … What of the future? If Britain and the Dominions can help to win the war, they have an undoubted right and duty to

help in winning the peace. Even more than during the last war the Dominions have earned the right to be heard in planning for the peace. They have something of value to contribute. They will help to carry out the objectives of the United Nations. They will also help to perpetuate the unity and solidarity of the British Commonwealth of Nations.'

15 For 'in both substance and style', see: Christopher Waters, 'Creating a Tradition: The Foreign Policy of the Curtin and Chifley Labor Governments' in David Lee & Christopher Waters (eds), *Evatt to Evans: The Labor Tradition in Australian Foreign Policy* (Allen & Unwin: Sydney, 1997), p. 35. For the policy emphasis, see: Norman Harper & David Sissons, *Australia and the United Nations* (Manhattan Publishing Company: New York, 1959), p. 34.

16 ibid., p. 43.

17 Nicholas Greet, 'Australian Policy towards the Emergent United Nations Organization 1944–1945: The role of Dr H. V. Evatt and his Department of External Affairs' (BA (Hons) thesis, Flinders University, Adelaide 1990), p. 15.

18 Greet, p. 15, citing Evatt to Curtin Cablegram 12.5.44 in *Documents on Australian Foreign Policy,* vol. 7, p. 288.

19 Greet, p. 16; Ross, pp. 356–7; P. G. Edwards, p. 163.

20 Evatt, 'Ministerial Statement', House of Representatives, 14 October 1944, in H. V. Evatt, *Foreign Policy of Australia: Speeches by the Rt Honourable H.V. Evatt MP* (Angus & Robertson: Sydney, 1945), p. 147.

21 C. W. P. Waters, *Anglo Australian Diplomacy 1945–1949: Labour Governments in Conflict* (PhD thesis, University of New South Wales, Australian Defence Force Academy, 1990), p. x.

22 Buckley et al, pp. 186ff and quote from p. 195; an excellent discussion of the comprehensive nature of the Curtin government's social and economic post-war reconstruction plans can be found in John Edwards, *Curtin's Gift: Reinterpreting Australia's Greatest Prime Minister* (Allen & Unwin: Sydney, 2005).

23 John Curtin, 'Policy Speech', 26 July 1943, cited in Lloyd Ross, pp. 326ff.

24 H. V. Evatt 'Australia's Future Role in the Pacific' published in the Sydney *Daily Telegraph* 18 August 1943, cited in Evatt, *Foreign Policy of Australia,* p. 133.

25 Amos Yoder, *The Evolution of the United Nations System* (2nd edn) (Taylor & Francis: Washington D.C., 1993), pp. 8, 13; Edward Luck, *UN Security Council: Practice and Promise* (Routledge: London, 2006), p. 24.

26 Quoted in T.R. Smith, *South Pacific Commission: An Analysis after Twenty-Five Years* (Price Milburn: Wellington, 1972), pp. 28–9.

27 'A Broadcast Talk by the AG and Minister for External Affairs, Dr Evatt, from Station 2UE and associate stations', Sunday 10/1/43 (Evatt Collection: Speeches and Statements).

28 'Labour Movements and the War: An Address by Dr Evatt at the British Labour Party Conference 25 May 1942' in Evatt, *Foreign Policy of Australia,* p. 63.

29 The preamble to the UN Charter begins: 'We the peoples of the United
Nations determined to save succeeding generations from the scourge of war,
which twice in our lifetime has brought untold sorrow to mankind, and to reaffirm
faith in fundamental human rights, in the dignity and worth of the human person,
in the equal rights of men and women and of nations large and small, and to
establish conditions under which justice and respect for the obligations arising
from treaties and other sources of international law can be maintained'.

2 – The birth of the UN

1 For example, Franklin Roosevelt unveiled plans for a new universal organisation
before the US Congress in 1943; see Kirsten Sellars, *The Rise and Rise of Human
Rights* (Sutton Publishing: Stroud, 2002), p. xi.
2 W. J. Hudson, *Australia and the New World Order: Evatt at San Francisco, 1945*
(Australian National University: Canberra, 1993), p. 7.
3 ibid., pp 7–11; see also Luck, pp. 68–70.
4 Hudson, p. 19; Buckley et al, pp. 227ff, 229, 233; Evatt/Forde report on the
UNCIO Conference (Evatt Collection: Conference on International Organisation
San Francisco).
5 Hudson, pp. 26–7, 32–3.
6 ibid., pp. 26–7.
7 ibid., pp. 34–5, referring to Department of External Affairs 'Notes on San Francisco
Conference' 28 February 1945 AA: A1066 H 45/775; see also Luck, pp. 112–3.
8 'The only true basis of enduring peace is the willing cooperation of free peoples in
a world in which, relieved of the menace of aggression, all may enjoy economic and
social security', UN Website   www.un.org/aboutun/charter/
9 'The Post-war Settlement in the Pacific', address delivered by Dr H. V. Evatt at
the Overseas Press Club, New York, 28 April 1943, cited in John Plant, 'The
origins and development of Australia's policy and posture at the United Nations
Conference on International Organization, San Francisco, 1945' (PhD thesis,
Australian National University, 1967), p. 405.
10 H. V. Evatt, 'Australia and America: University of California Charter Address
March 1945' in H. V. Evatt, *Australia in World Affairs* (Angus & Robertson: Sydney,
1946), p. 15.
11 Hudson, pp. 38–9.
12 ibid., pp. 38–9; see also Day, p. 566.
13 ibid., p. 40; a more complete discussion and description of the internal tensions
in the delegation can be found in Plant, pp. 239ff; P.G. Edwards, pp. 165–6.
14 Hudson quotes Evatt's telegram to Beasley: 'what Curtin told me at the last was
that I should recognise Forde's seniority but at the same time Forde must
recognise that all the matters at the conference related to foreign affairs and that
these were my primary responsibility … this seemed an almost impossible plan',

Evatt to Beasley, 1 May 1945 *Documents on Australian Foreign Policy*, vol. 8, p.155, cited in Hudson, p. 41. Plant, pp. 209–12.
15 ibid., p. 211; P.G. Edwards, p. 166.
16 Greet, p. 32.
17 Evatt/Forde UNCIO Conference Report.
18 Yoder, p. 29.
19 H. V. Evatt, 'Untitled Draft' (Evatt Collection: Publications, UN), pp. 21–2.
20 ibid., p. 5.5.
21 ibid., p. 5.6.
22 Plant, p. 409.
23 David Lee, 'The Curtin and Chifley Governments, Liberal Internationalism and World Organisation', in Lee & Waters, p. 50; Waters, 'Creating a Tradition', p. 38.
24 'Circular: The Australian Parliament — Attitudes towards the UNO 1944–1952' (Evatt Collection: UN Miscellaneous); Harper & Sissons, pp. 45–6 citing *Documents of the United Nations Conference on International Organisation, San Francisco 1945* (New York: United Nations Information Organizations, 1945), vol. 3, pp. 543ff; H. V. Evatt 'Australia and the United Nations', Speech in the Australian Parliament 30 August 1945, in Evatt, *Australia in World Affairs,* pp. 45–6.
25 Greet, p. 43, citing Paul Hasluck 'Australia and the Formation of the United Nations', *Royal Australian Historical Society, Journal and Proceedings*, XL, III, p, 173; P. G. Edwards, p. 168.
26 Harper & Sissons, p. 48.
27 Plant, p. 338.
28 Lee, 'Liberal Internationalism', p. 50.
29 Evatt/Forde UNCIO report.
30 Greet, p. 44; Evatt/Forde UNCIO report; Evatt Collection Cablegram from Forde and Evatt to Curtin, 28 April 1945 (Evatt Collection: Conference on International Organisation San Francisco).
31 Evatt/Forde UNCIO report.
32 Plant, pp. 316ff. See also: Harper & Sissons, p. 79.
33 Renouf, pp. 235–6.
34 Kenneth Bailey cited in Buckley et al, p. 207.
35 Smith, p. 28.
36 Renouf, p. 256.
37 Waters, *Anglo Australian Diplomacy,* p. 233.
38 Plant, p. 338.
39 ibid., pp. 353–4.
40 McMullin, p. 196.
41 Lee, 'Liberal Internationalism', p. 50.
42 Yoder, p. 30 ; Stanley Meisler, *United Nations: The First Fifty Years* (The Atlantic Monthly Press: New York, 1995), p. 18.
43 Lee, 'Liberal Internationalism', p. 51.

44 ibid., p. 50.
45 ibid., p. 51; Luck, p. 14; see also Harper & Sissons, p. 50.
46 Harper & Sissons, pp. 52–3; also Evatt/Forde UNCIO report which makes the same claim that all countries which abstained supported the amendment, and so did a number who voted no.
47 Lee, 'Liberal Internationalism', p. 51.
48 Yoder, p. 30; see also information in Meisler, p. 19.
49 A. Roberts & B. Kingsbury (eds), *United Nations, Divided World: The UN's Roles in International Relations* (2nd edn) (Clarendon Press: Oxford, 1993), p. 31.
50 H. V. Evatt, 'The World Situation Today' lecture at the Australian Institute of Political Science Winter Forum, 1948 (Evatt Collection: Speeches and Statements); Evatt expressed similar concerns in a statement on international affairs tabled in the House of Representatives on 11 March 1948.
51 Lee, 'Liberal Internationalism', p. 51.
52 Renouf, p. 219; The 'Post-war Reconstruction and Democratic Rights' referendum on 4 July 1944 was to give the Commonwealth power, for a period of five years, to legislate on matters such as national health, family allowances, rehabilitation for returned soldiers and 'the people of the Aboriginal race'. It was defeated, as were subsequent Labor government referendums 'Organised Marketing of Primary Products and Industrial Employment' in 1946, and 'Rent and Prices' in 1948. The only successful referendum in the years of the Curtin-Chifley governments was the 'Social Services' referendum in 1946.
53 Luck, p 15; Plant, pp. 282–4; Evatt/Forde report on UNCIO.
54 Lee, 'Liberal Internationalism', p. 51.
55 ibid., p. 52 citing Commonwealth Government to Cranborne, 5 September 1944 *Documents on Australian Foreign Policy,* vol. 8, p. 521.
56 Harper & Sissons, p. 59.
57 ibid., p. 57.
58 Lee, 'Liberal Internationalism', p. 52, citing Hudson, pp. 93–4; Evatt/Forde report on UNCIO; Harper & Sissons, p. 58.
59 Lee, 'Liberal Internationalism', pp. 52–3; see also Yoder, p. 30; Plant, pp. 391–5.
60 Lee, 'Liberal Internationalism', p. 53.
61 Harper & Sissons, pp. 59, 80.
62 Lee, 'Liberal Internationalism', p. 60.
63 Commonwealth Parliamentary Debates (*Hansard*) vol. 202, 21 June 1949, pp. 1212–26.
64 For a more complete discussion of the implications of Domestic Jurisdiction and the UN, see J. E. S. Fawcett, 'Human Rights and Domestic Jurisdiction', in Evan Luard (ed), *The International Protection of Human Rights* (Frederick A. Praeger: New York, 1967), pp. 286–90.
65 National Archives: [AA : A1066, H45/771/1] 91 Forde and Evatt to Chifley Cablegram E34 SAN FRANCISCO, 18 May 1945, 11.08 p.m.

66 National Archives: [AA : A1066, H45/771/1] 104 Evatt to External Affairs Cablegram E42 SAN FRANCISCO, 6 June 1945, 9.32 p.m; see also Evatt/Forde UNCIO report.

67 Plant, p. 366. Harper & Sissons, pp 63–4; Tennant, p. 175.

68 McMullin, pp. 46–7, 310.

69 Harper & Sissons, p. 144.

70 Sellars, p. 7.

71 C. A. Macartney 'League of Nations' Protection of Minority Rights', in Luard, p. 23.

72 United Nations Charter, 2.7.

73 Harper & Sissons, pp. 145, 175–6.

74 ibid., pp. 154–5.

75 Buckley et al, p. 306.

76 Harper & Sissons, pp. 164–5; see, for example, positions on South Africa, where Australia's position on the applicability of the Charter changed from vote to vote, and contradictory positions on human rights violations in Hungary, Bulgaria and Romania and on the repressive regime in Spain. Harper & Sissons, pp. 148ff, 153ff.

77 Yoder, p. 129.

78 Buckley et al, pp. 302ff; Harper & Sissons, pp. 146ff.

79 W. J. Hudson, *Australia and the Colonial Question at the United Nations* (Sydney University Press: Sydney 1970), p. 147.

80 ibid., p. 13.

81 Cited in Evan Luard, 'Promotion of Human Rights by UN Political Bodies', in Luard, p. 141.

82 H. V. Evatt 'Statement on Trusteeship' (Evatt Collection: UN – Trusteeship).

83 Cablegram from Chifley 8 June 1945 to Evatt and Forde (Evatt Collection: Conference on International Organisation San Francisco).

84 W. J. Hudson, *Australia and the New World Order: Evatt at San Francisco, 1945,* pp. 44–5; Evatt/Forde UNCIO Report; Harper and Sissons, p. 49.

85 Harper & Sissons, p. 70; Plant, p 367; Evatt/Forde report on UNCIO Conference; Tennant, p. 169; Hudson, *Australia and the Colonial Question,* p. 25.

86 Harper & Sissons, p. 72; Plant, pp. 367–8.

87 Harper & Sissons, pp. 77, 83; Evatt 'Untitled document' (Evatt Collection United Nations — Committees — Findings of General Assembly); Evatt 'Statement on Trusteeship'; Hudson, *Australia and the Colonial Question,* pp. 4. 29, 164; Tennant, pp. 197–8

88 Compare, for example, the 22-year gestation of the Declaration on the Rights of Indigenous Peoples.

89 Roberts & Kingsbury, 'Introduction', in Roberts & Kingsbury, p. 48.

90 ibid., p. 49.

91 Rosemary Righter, *Utopia Lost: The United Nations and World Order* (Twentieth Century Fund Press: New York, 1995), pp. 40–1.

92 Lee, 'Liberal Internationalism', pp 53–4.

93 Cited in Plant, p. 395.
94 H. V. Evatt Cablegram to Chifley, Beasley and Makin 24 June 1945 (Evatt Collection: UN: Conference on International Organisation: Cables).
95 Harper & Sissons, pp. 78–9 citing Australian delegation report on UNCIO, p. 15.
96 ibid., pp. 78–9.
97 Draft Statement by Minister for External Affairs, 13 September 1946, EC External Affairs – US.
98 ibid.
99 ibid.

3 – The UN in practice

1 David Day, *Chifley* (Harper Collins: Sydney, 2001), p. 436.
2 Renouf, p. 256.
3 ibid., pp. 235–7.
4 Faulkner & Macintyre, 'Introduction' p. xxix.
5 'John Curtin: A Labor Life', Eighth John Curtin Prime Ministerial Library Anniversary Lecture marking the 61st anniversary of John Curtin's death, 5 July 2006, presented by the Hon. John Faulkner, Senator for NSW.
6 Lawrence W. Maher, 'Half Light between War and Peace: Herbert Vere Evatt, the Rule of International Law and the Corfu Channel Case' *Australian Journal of Legal History*, 3, p. 65, citing Geoffrey Sawyer 'The United Nations', in G. Greenwood & N. Harper (eds), *Australia in World Affairs 1950–1955*, (Melbourne: FW Cheshire, 1957).
7 Buckley et al, p. 305.
8 Waters, 'Creating a Tradition', p. 40; Lee, 'Liberal Internationalism', p. 48.
9 Waters, 'Creating a Tradition', p. 40; this argument is also made by Lee, 'Liberal Internationalism', p. 48.
10 Waters, 'Creating a Tradition', p. 41.
11 'Report no 1 from Australian Delegation to Conference of Paris' (Evatt Collection United Nations Paris Peace Conference); Waters, *Anglo Australian Diplomacy*, p. 103.
12 C. W. P. Waters, 'Voices in the Wilderness: H.V. Evatt and the European Peace Settlement, 1945–1947', p. 62, in David Day, *Brave New World: Dr. H. V. Evatt and Australian foreign policy, 1941–1949*, (University of Queensland Press: St Lucia, 1996).
13 'Draft Statement by Minister for External Affairs', 13 September 1946 — (Evatt Collection — External Affairs — US).
14 Buckley et al, p. 303; Waters, *Anglo Australian Diplomacy*, p. 205.
15 Waters, 'Creating a Tradition', p. 40; see also Lee, 'Liberal Internationalism', p. 48.
16 Renouf, p. 239.
17 Waters, 'Creating a Tradition', p. 40; Lee, 'Liberal Internationalism', p. 48.
18 Harper & Sissons, p. 53.

19 H. V. Evatt, 'A Review of International Affairs', Statement of Foreign Affairs to
the Australian House of Representatives in Evatt, *Australia in World Affairs*, p. 161.
20 Telegram W 40 Sydney Sub 58 5–3 P (Evatt Collection, UN Security Council).
21 Waters, *Anglo Australian Diplomacy*, p. 233.
22 'Circular: The Australian Parliament — Attitudes Towards the UNO 1944–52'
(Evatt Collection: UN Miscellaneous), citing CPD vol. 186, 13 March 1946, p. 192.
23 Lee, 'Liberal Internationalism', p. 56, citing Waters, 'Australia, the Security
Council and the Iranian Crisis of 1946: Liberal Internationalism in Practice',
Australian Journal of Political Science, vol. 28, no. 1, March 1993, pp. 83–97; Lee,
'Liberal Internationalism', p. 56, citing Evatt to Makin 23 June 1945, *Documents on
Australian Foreign Policy,* vol. VIII, p. 230.
24 Evan Luard, 'Promotion of Human Rights by UN Political Bodies', in Luard, p. 135.
25 Evatt Collection United Nations — Committees — Findings of General
Assembly; see also H. V. Evatt, *The United Nations* (Oxford University Press:
London, 1948), pp. 56–71.
26 Timothy McCormack, 'H V Evatt at San Francisco: A Lasting Contribution to
International Law' *Australian Year Book of International Law*, vol. 13, 1992, p. 98.
27 Lee, 'Liberal internationalism', pp. 58.
28 ibid.
29 ibid., pp. 316–7.
30 Renouf, pp. 240–1.
31 Yoder, pp. 96–7.
32 H. V. Evatt, 'Analysis of the relationship between organized measures for the
international control of atomic energy and the united nations organisation
(Particularly the Security Council)', submitted to the Atomic Energy Commission
July 8 1946 (Evatt Collection: AEC).
33 ibid; see also H. V. Evatt, 'Atomic Energy Commission: Speech by the
Chairman', 25 June 1946 (Evatt Collection: AEC).
34 H. V. Evatt, 'The World Situation Today'.
35 Yoder, p. 50.
36 Marie Kawaja, 'H.V. Evatt and The Palestine Question', *The Life and Work of Dr
H.V. Evatt: A Weekend Conference at Bond University July 14–15 1990,* Evatt
Collection; Dr H V Evatt, 'Peace — How Can It Be Achieved' — Address to the
Nation Associates 7th April 1949 — (Evatt Collection: UN Miscellaneous);
Buckley et al, p. 311.
37 Renouf, p. 246; Buckley et al, p. 311.
38 Buckley et al, p. 311.
39 Renouf, p. 246; Buckley et al, p. 311.
40 ibid., p. 312; Evatt's own accounts of these events can be found in his Dr H V
Evatt, 'Peace — How Can It Be Achieved' and in H. V. Evatt 'The World
Situation Today', while a very detailed account of the work of the committee can

be found in Evatt's 'Statement on International Affairs' tabled in the House of Representatives on Thursday 11 March 1948.
41 Telegraph 27 Nov 1947 to Mr Trygvie Lie and M. Cordier, UN Secretariat (Evatt Collection: UN Miscellaneous).
42 Renouf, p. 246; Buckley et al, p. 311.
43 ibid., p. 312.
44 ibid.
45 Telegraph 27 Nov 1947 to Mr Trygvie Lie and M Cordier, UN Secretariat (Evatt Collection: UN Miscellaneous).
46 Buckley et al, p. 312. These basic facts are also described in Yoder, pp. 50–1.
47 'The Work of the Australian Delegation to the Third Session of the General Assembly' (Evatt Collection United Nations — Australian Delegation to the General Assembly).
48 Evatt, 'The World Situation Today'.
49 Evatt, 'Peace — How Can It Be Achieved'.

4 – Human rights

1 Yoder, pp. 2–3.
2 Jack Donnelly, *International Human Rights* (2nd ed) (Westview Press: Boulder Colorado, 1998), p. 5; Evan Luard, 'The Origins of International Concern over Human Rights', in Luard, p. 14; John P. Humphrey, 'The UN Charter and the Universal Declaration of Human Rights', in Luard, p. 39.
3 Tony Evans, *The Politics of Human Rights* (2nd ed) (Pluto Press: London, 2005), pp. 12–13.
4 Tom J. Farer & Felice Gaer, 'The UN and Human Rights', in Roberts & Kingsbury, p. 245; Humphrey, p. 40.
5 Harper & Sissons, p, 79, citing Evatt, *Australia in World Affairs*, p. 54.
6 ibid.
7 ibid., p. 64.
8 Buckley et al, pp. 303–4.
9 Lee, 'Liberal Internationalism', p. 54.
10 Harper & Sissons, p. 135.
11 Lee, 'Liberal Internationalism', p. 54.
12 Harper & Sissons, p. 253.
13 Tennant, pp. 69–70.
14 Harper & Sissons, p. 254.
15 ibid., p. 68.
16 John Burton, 'A Human Component: The Failure of the Labor Tradition', in Lee & Waters, p. 24; Harper & Sissons, p. 68.
17 Lee, 'Liberal Internationalism', p. 54; Edwards, pp. 170–1.
18 Cablegram from Evatt in San Francisco on 26 May 1945 to Beasley: Evatt concludes with characteristic lack of humility: 'I hope our distinguished colleagues will appreciate that this has not been achieved without persistent and unfailing

effort. I would respectfully suggest appropriate press statement.' (Evatt Collection: UN Conference on International Organisation San Francisco Cables).
19 Garry Woodard, 'Australia's Contribution to the Universal Declaration of Human Rights' (Evatt Collection: General Assembly).
20 As Faulkner said of Curtin, 'What distinguishes us from those who share some of Labor's goals without commitment to Labor's *cause* is our conviction that economic and industrial rights are as indispensable to a good society as civil and political rights. Working Australians need both freedom from want and freedom to speak to be full and equal citizens.' (*Curtin Anniversary Lecture*).
21 Sir Samuel Hoare, 'The UN Commission on Human Rights', in Luard, p. 59.
22 Humphrey, p. 47.
23 ibid., p. 48.
24 Woodard.
25 The Evatt Collection contains many detailed cablegrams between the Australian representatives and Evatt and his office covering almost all aspects of UN business in careful detail including stern warnings to 'carry out Australia's policy without deviation … I want fuller warning of what Australian representatives are to do and more strict adherence to my statement', Telegram to Hasluck from Evatt 5th August 1946 (Evatt Collection: AEC); and detailed instructions from Evatt regarding the Draft declaration and the drafting process (Evatt Collection: Cables).
26 L. Kramer & others (eds), *The Greats* (Angus & Robertson, Sydney, 1986), p. 242, cited in McMullin, p. 245.
27 'The Work of the Australian Delegation to the Third Session of the General Assembly' (Evatt Collection United Nations — Australian Delegation to the General Assembly).
28 ibid. p. 230. See Waters, *Anglo Australian Diplomacy,* (pp. 205ff), for an extensive discussion of Evatt as 'The Universal Conciliator'.
29 Evatt Collection: UN Miscellaneous.
30 'The Work of the Australian Delegation to the Third Session of the General Assembly'.
31 General Assembly, Official Records, 3rd Sess, 1st part, 181st Plenary Mtg, 10 December 1948, p. 875, cited in Harper and Sissons, p. 255.
32 Yoder, p.129.
33 Luard, 'Conclusions', in Luard, p. 311.
34 ibid.
35 Righter, p. 82.
36 The Universal Declaration can be found online at: www.un.org/Overview/rights.html
37 www.un.org/rights/morerights.htm
38 Tony Evans, p. 7; Ian Russell, 'Australia's Human Rights Policy: From Evatt to Evans', in Ian Russell, Peter Van Ness, Beng-Huat Chua, *Australia's Human Rights Diplomacy* (Australian Foreign Policy Papers: Canberra 1992), p. 9.

39 Tony Evans, p. 1, citing UNDP, 1994 UNDP Human Development Report.
40 Tony Evans, pp. 12–13.
41 Humphrey, p. 49, citing L. M. Goodrich, *The United Nations* (New York 1959), p. 324.
42 Humphrey, p. 51.
43 H. V. Evatt, 'Speech by Herbert V. Evatt President of the General Assembly of the United Nations to M. Vincent Auriol, Mr Schuman and The French Government at the Elysee Palace 11 December 1948' (Evatt Collection: United Nations — Australian Delegation to the General Assembly).

5 – Legacy

1 Day, *Chifley*, pp. 481ff.
2 Draft Telegram to G Logie Smith, Geelong College, Geelong (Evatt Collection: UN Festival Geelong).
3 For more detailed discussion of the Split and Evatt's behaviour before and during, see: Brian Costar, Peter Love & Paul Strangio (eds), *The Great Labor Schism: A Retrospective* (Scribe Publications: Melbourne, 2005); Also: McMullin; Faulkner & Macintyre.
4 Sean Scalmer discusses this period of Evatt's career in 'Crisis to Crisis: 1950–66' in Faulkner & Macintyre, pp. 93–8.
5 Renouf, p. 235.
6 C. Meigs, *The Great Design: Men and Events in the United Nations from 1945 to 1963*, Little, Brown: Boston, 1964, pp. 49–50 cited in McCormack, p. 105.
7 Gareth Evans, *The Future of the United Nations: An Australian Perspective*, United Nations Association of Australia Conference, National Press Club, Canberra, 1 September 1995.
8 Renouf, pp. 239–240.
9 ibid., p. 256.
10 Buckley et al, p. 32.
11 H. V. Evatt, 'The Smaller Powers and UNO', Address given at Dutch Treat Club, New York, 27 November 1945' in Evatt, *Australia in World Affairs*, p. 97.
12 Roberts & Kingsbury, 'Introduction', pp. 14–5.
13 ibid., p. 19.
14 Geoffrey Bolton, 'Evatt, Herbert Vere (Bert) (1894 - 1965)', *Australian Dictionary of Biography*, vol. 14 (Melbourne University Press: Melbourne, 1996), pp. 108–14; see also Waters, *Anglo Australian Diplomacy*, pp. 205ff.
15 H. V. Evatt, 'Statement written for NEA News Service' (Evatt Collection: UN Miscellaneous).
16 H. V. Evatt, 'The World Situation Today'.
17 'The United Nations and Human Welfare', address by H. V. Evatt to the Australian National Committee for the United Nations, Brisbane, 8 November 1949 (Evatt Collection: UN Miscellaneous).
18 Evatt, 'Statement written for NEA News Service'.

Bibliography

This work is not meant to break new ground, but rather to provide a readily accessible introduction to the story of Evatt and the United Nations. I have focused on Evatt's public and professional statements, documents and actions. Herbert Vere 'Doc' Evatt remains a controversial figure in Australian history. I hope that readers will draw their own conclusions about his political work in the 1940s based on what he did and said.

The United Nations has also been subject to controversy. Both the UN and Evatt have been subject to both laudatory and vitriolic analyses. In drawing together this portrait of Evatt's role in the foundation of the UN and in shaping its structures and purposes, I have relied most heavily on those secondary sources that chart a course between the two extremes. I have also been fortunate enough to have access to the Evatt Collection held at Flinders University Library. The collection holds a wealth of documents generated by and collected by Evatt himself. Not all of these documents were clearly identified by Evatt, and some are multiple drafts of subsequently published documents.

While I am sure some future historian will have a field day comparing different drafts and reaching conclusions about the development of Evatt's opinions and the role played by his staff and colleagues, my focus on him as public figure led me to draw, wherever possible, on published documents and statements rather than original manuscripts. There are, however, a number of documents in the Evatt Collection and not available elsewhere which provide valuable insight into Evatt's work and how he wished it to be viewed, and which can be characterised as reliable — published copies of speeches he gave which have not survived elsewhere, newspaper clippings and articles containing quotes and interviews with Evatt, memos circulated at the UN Conference and copies of telegrams sent to and received from his staff and his political colleagues.

For readers interested in Evatt's life, the biography by Ken Buckley, Barbara Dale and Wayne Williams, *Doc Evatt: Patriot, Internationalist, Fighter and Scholar,* provides a good starting point. W. J. Hudson's *Australia and the New World Order: Evatt at San Francisco, 1945* and David Day's *Brave New World: Dr H.V. Evatt and Australian foreign policy, 1941-1949* provide strong and detailed overviews of Evatt's role in the early years of the United Nations. Norman Harper and David Sissons, in *Australia and the United Nations*, place Australia's UN policy in a broader context and carry the story beyond the years of Evatt's involvement. The main sources consulted are below.

Beaumont, Joan, Waters, Christopher, Lowe, David & Woodard, Garry, *Ministers, Mandarins and Diplomats: Australia Foreign Policy Making, 1941–1969* (Melbourne University Press: Melbourne, 2003).

Bolton, Geoffrey, 'Evatt, Herbert Vere (Bert) (1894-1965)', *Australian Dictionary of Biography*, vol. 14 (Melbourne University Press: Melbourne, 1996), pp. 108-14.

——, *The Oxford History of Australia, Volume 5: The Middle Way 1942-1995* (2nd edition) (Oxford University Press: Melbourne, 1996).

Buckley, Ken, Dale, Barbara & Williams, Wayne, *Doc Evatt: Patriot, Internationalist, Fighter and Scholar* (Longman Cheshire: Melbourne, 1994).

Cain, Frank, *Jack Lang and the Great Depression* (Australian Scholarly Publishing: Melbourne, 2005).

Costar, Brian, Love, Peter & Strangio, Paul (eds), *The Great Labor Schism: A Retrospective* (Scribe: Melbourne, 2005).

Crockett, Peter, *Evatt: A Life* (OUP: Melbourne, 1993).

Day, David, *Brave New World: Dr H.V. Evatt and Australian Foreign Policy, 1941-1949* (University of Queensland Press: St Lucia, 1996).

——, *Chifley* (Harper Collins: Sydney, 2001).

——, *John Curtin: A Life* (Harper Collins: Sydney, 1999).

Donnelly, Jack, *International Human Rights* (2nd edition) (Westview Press: Boulder Colorado, 1998).

Edwards, John, *Curtin's Gift: Reinterpreting Australia's Greatest Prime Minister* (Allen & Unwin: Sydney, 2005).

Edwards, P. G., *Prime Ministers and Diplomats: the Making of Australian Foreign Policy* (Oxford University Press: Melbourne, 1983).

Evans, Tony, *The Politics of Human Rights* (2nd edition) (Pluto Press: London, 2005).

Evatt, H. V., 'International Affairs – Statement prepared by Minister for External Affairs', Tabled in the House of Representatives – 11 March 1948 NAA: A 1838/1, 568/8 PT2B.

——, *Australia in World Affairs* (Angus & Robertson: Sydney, 1946).

——, *Foreign Policy of Australia: Speeches* (Angus & Robertson: Sydney, 1945).

——, *The United Nations* (Oxford University Press: London, 1948)

Fabian Society, *The 25th Anniversary Year of the UN and a Special Tribute to Dr Evatt* (Fabian Society of Queensland Publication: Brisbane, 1970).

Faulkner, John & Macintyre, Stuart (eds), *True Believers: The Story of the Federal Parliamentary Labor Party* (Allen & Unwin: Sydney, 2001).

Freudenberg, Graham, *Cause for Power: The Official History of the New South Wales Branch of the Australian Labor Party* (Pluto Press: Sydney, 1991).

Greet, Nicholas, 'Australian Policy towards the Emergent United Nations Organization 1944-1945: The Role of Dr H. V. Evatt and his Department of External Affairs', (thesis submitted for the honours degree of Bachelor of Arts, Flinders University, 1990).

Harper, Norman & Sissons, David, *Australia and the United Nations* (Manhattan Publishing Co: New York, 1959).

70

Hudson, W. J., *Australia and the Colonial Question at the United Nations* (Sydney University Press: Sydney, 1970).

——, *Australia and the New World Order: Evatt at San Francisco, 1945* (ANU: Canberra, 1993).

Lee, David & Waters, Christopher (eds), *Evatt to Evans: The Labor Tradition in Australian Foreign Policy* (Allen & Unwin: Sydney, 1997).

Luard, Evan (ed.), *The International Protection of Human Rights* (Frederick A. Praeger Publishers: New York, 1967).

Luck, Edward C., *UN Security Council: Practice and Promise* (Routledge: London, 2006).

Maher, Lawrence W., 'Half Light Between War and Peace: Herbert Vere Evatt, The Rule of International Law and the Corfu Channel Case', *Australian Journal of Legal History* 2005, pp 47-83.

McCormack, Timothy, 'H. V. Evatt at San Francisco: A Lasting Contribution to International Law', *Australian Year Book of International Law*, vol. 13, 1992, pp. 89-105.

McMullin, Ross, *The Light on the Hill: The Australian Labor Party 1891- 1991* (OUP: Melbourne: 1991).

Meisler, Stanley, *United Nations: The First Fifty Years* (Atlantic Monthly Press: New York, 1995).

Plant, John David Edward, 'The origins and development of Australia's policy and posture at the United Nations Conference on International Organization, San Francisco, 1945' (thesis submitted for the degree of Doctor of Philosophy: Australian National University, 1967).

Renouf, Alan, *Let Justice Be Done: The Foreign Policy of Dr H. V. Evatt* (University of Queensland Press: St Lucia,1983).

Righter, Rosemary, *Utopia Lost: The United Nations and World Order* (Twentieth Century Fund Press: New York, 1995).

Roberts, Adam & Kingsbury, Benedict (eds), *United Nations, Divided World: The UN's Roles in International Relations* (2nd edition) (Clarendon Press: Oxford, 1993).

Ross, Lloyd, *John Curtin: A Biography* (Macmillan Company of Australia: Melbourne, 1977).

Russel, Ian, Van Ness, Peter & Chua, Beng-Huat, *Australia's Human Rights Diplomacy* (Australian Foreign Policy Papers: Canberra, 1992).

Sellars, Kirsten, *The Rise and Rise of Human Rights* (Sutton Publishing: Stroud, 2002).

Smith, T. R., *South Pacific Commission: An analysis after twenty-five years* (Price Milburn: Wellington, 1972).

Tennant, Kylie, *Evatt: Politics and Justice* (Angus & Robertson: Sydney, 1970).

Waters, C.W.P., 'Anglo Australian Diplomacy 1945-1949: Labour Governments in Conflict' (thesis submitted for the degree of Doctor of Philosophy, University of New South Wales, Australian Defence Force Academy, 1990).

Yoder, Amos, *The Evolution of the United Nations System* (2nd edition) (Taylor & Francis: Washington D.C., 1993).

72

About the Evatt Foundation

The Herbert Vere Evatt
Memorial Foundation
Incorporated was established
in 1979 with the aim of
advancing the highest ideals
of the labour movement,
such as equality,
participation, social justice
and human rights.

The Foundation pursues its
objectives by promoting:
• research and discussion of
public issues;
• an awareness of social,
political and economic
aspects of Australian life;
• academic and applied
research for trade unions, the
labour movement and other
community organisations;
• education and vocational
training;
• young artists in Australia.

Office Bearers in 2008

President: Christopher Sheil
Vice President: Ron Dyer
Vice President: Penny Sharpe
Secretary: Chris Gambian

Executive Committee

Bruce Childs
Jeannette McHugh
Susan Tracey
Richard Gartrell
Frank Stilwell
Warwick McDonald
Mark McGrath
Fay Gervasoni
Mel Gatfield

Mailing Address

The Evatt Foundation
Main Quadrangle (A14)
University of Sydney
Sydney NSW Australia 2000

Office Location

Level 1, Sydney Trades Hall
4–10 Goulburn Street,
Sydney, Australia

Other contact details

Phone: (61 2) 8090 1170
Fax: (61 2) 8090 1171
E-mail:
secretary@evatt.usyd.edu.au
Website: evatt.org.au

About this publication

In 2007 the Evatt Foundation invited applications from suitably qualified scholars to research and write a monograph on Dr Evatt and the United Nations. The work was to be undertaken for publication on the 60th anniversary of his election as President of the General Assembly and the adoption and proclamation of the Universal Declaration of Human Rights in 2008.

Acknowledgements

The author thanks Lorraine Burdett, Kate Deverall, Deirdre McKeown and Dy Spooner for their encouragement, support and assistance throughout the project.

The work was edited by Christopher Sheil. The production was assisted by Jeannette McHugh, Ron Dyer, Bruce Childs and Chris Gambian.

Thanks to Susan Murray-Smith and Agata Mrva-Montoya at Sydney University Press.

All photographs are from the Evatt Collection. Thanks to Gillian Dooley, Special Collections Librarian, Flinders University, Adelaide, South Australia.